Babies All Wrapped Up

by Dr Claire Winstanley

All content within this book is provided for general information only, and should not be treated as a substitute for the medical advice of your own doctor or any other health care professional. The book is not responsible or liable for any diagnosis made by a user based on the content of this book. This book is not liable for the contents of any external internet sites listed, nor does it endorse any commercial product or service mentioned or advised on any of the sites. Always consult your own GP if you are in any way concerned about your or your baby's health.

Babies All Wrapped Up - Second Edition September 2012

ISBN 978-0-9572491-1-0

Copyright Claire Winstanley 2012

Published in the UK by DragonWeb Publishing Ltd

73 Greville Road, Bristol BS3 1LE

www.DragonWebPublishing.com

Cover photo Milan Jurek www.sxc.hu

Illustrations by Elinor B. Greenacre

www.elinordesigns.co.uk

About Claire

I am a GP currently based in Bristol and mother to 3 young children. My interests within Medicine are diverse and amongst other things have led me into a fascination with all alternative therapies, Acupuncture and Chinese Herbal Medicine (Diploma). I am greatly interested in diet also and how it affects a person's health and wellbeing. Above all, I enjoy the variety general practice offers and the challenges it presents.

I have written this book as after the birth of my first child, I sat on my hospital bed and felt totally overwhelmed. Although I had read some baby books I still felt bereft of decent information; even as a practising GP!

This is the book I wanted and needed when I sat there wondering what to do next! It prepares the mother for what happens to her own body just after the birth - a time few people talk about. This book gives parents options on how to look after the newborn and young baby from the offset.

We are all so different in the way we think and live our lives, I wanted to produce a book giving parents the intrinsic guidelines so they can then choose how to add their own tailored form of care from thereon in.

Acknowledgements

I would like to thank Dr Georgina Selby who is a Paediatric specialist in Diabetes and Endocrinology at Bristol Children's Hospital. Her advice with regard to the paediatric side of the book was very helpful with up to date medical thinking and advice. Linda Hicken - senior midwife at Southmead Hospital in Bristol, was wonderful with her feedback as an experienced midwife; especially informing me that babies are born/ birthed not delivered (pizzas and take-a-ways are delivered)! Helen Archer is a Senior Health Visitor in Bristol and was also superb with her input from a Health Visitors' point of view especially with the advice on bedding and temperature control in the cot.

Also Dr Joanna Walsh, MRCP (paeds) MRCGP and Dr Charlotte Dawson, SpR Clinical Biochemistry at Bristol Royal Infirmary, for their helpful knowlegde and support. Debbie Chase, Senior Staff Nurse at Bristol Childrens Hospital, Pricilla Moxey, Staff Nurse at the Bristol Childrens Hospital and Joanna Westlake all really helped me with the book using their valuable experience.

A collective 'thank you' also goes to Jane Welham, Sarah Burch, Fiona Hester, Jacqueline Berridge, Kate Duree, Judy Barker, Sarah Bonnett and Amanda Welch for all their support and feedback while writing this. They have all been wonderfully encouraging and sharing advice that really mattered to them or asking me to answer questions for them.

Sarah Coleman added valuable contribution to the book with her excellent editorial advice helping me to focus on each title to make it as concise as possible.

The beautiful illustrations by Elinor Greenacre are delightful and have added warmth to our second edition.

A big thank you is also needed to Tessa-Lynne Davies and Jonathan Jenkins for publishing this book. It is not a simple task!

CONTENTS

Detailed Contents

INTRODUCTION

This is the book I wish I'd had when I was sitting in St Thomas's hospital, overlooking the Houses of Parliament, holding my first baby. Suddenly I realised that, although as a GP I had lots of medical knowledge about babies, and I had read some books on babies, I still did not really know what to do with my own. I now have three children and I wanted to write a book filled with information and ideas so you can make your own decisions on what is best for you and your baby.

I have concentrated on what happens once your baby is born. Antenatal classes are really informative and help you to prepare for the birth of your baby – but once labour's over, you need to know what to do. I have aimed to give simple advice on how to cope and look after both your baby and yourself, from feeding to sleep and beyond. This book is for mothers, fathers, partners and primary carers. Because time is short and you're likely to be tired, I have kept it as concise as possible and only included information that you really need.

This book is full of suggestions and guidelines to help you as there is so much to learn once your baby is born. It is an incredibly steep learning-curve, and once you are alone at home it can be overwhelming.

There are sections on mothers' health, postnatal depression, the father's role and changes that take place for couples and single parents. As a GP I have been involved with many people who have struggled with health problems and emotional issues after the birth of their baby. It helps to be aware of some of the pitfalls in advance.

There are sections on medical advice to act as a reference guide to common and some less common ailments which is there to help not scare you. I have also included a section on dangers to consider in your home.

I have not talked about twins or babies with special needs specifically. However this book will help you in lots of practical areas of their care and also for you.

There is a huge change to your lifestyle when you have a baby. You are no longer in complete control of your life. You need to adapt your life to allow for this new member of the family. And however much you try to plan and prepare, your baby will dictate what happens next. If you can accept this, go with the flow and not fight the inevitable changes, you will enjoy it all so much more.

Having babies is a celebration of life, and I want to help you get the best out of this special time.

You have a natural maternal and paternal instinct. Trust it and use it.

1: PREPARING FOR YOUR BABY'S ARRIVAL

THE ESSENTIALS

Here's a checklist of the essentials that you will need, whether you plan to give birth at home or in a hospital:

For your baby
- Newborn nappies – 1 bag of 32. You'll be surprised how many you can go through in the early days.
- Cotton wool balls.
- Nappy sacks or bags.
- Bodysuits (cotton only) – buy 3 to 6.
- Sleep suits (cotton only, with feet unless very hot), or bundlers (like oversized nightshirts that tie up at the bottom – great when changing your baby at night as they just have a drawstring and no poppers) – minimum needed is 3.

- Hat – to keep warm or for the sun.
- Cardigan (depending on the temperature outside). If you prefer a jumper then buy one with buttons on the neck-line, as babies have large heads compared to the rest of them, making jumpers difficult to get on and off.
- All-in-one warm pramsuit if winter, ideally with gloves and feet attached as they fall off easily and little hands and feet get cold.
- Baby blanket.
- Muslins – useful if breast-feeding or for any possetting or vomiting – at least 6.
- Car seat, if you plan to drive home from hospital. The car seat needs a 'head hugger' to support your baby's head until it is about three months old.
- Otherwise a pram or pushchair that can lie flat, or a baby sling.

For you
If you plan to give birth in hospital, you will usually be in for six hours to three days after your baby is born, unless there are complications. So try to pack light!

- Wash bag – toothbrush, toothpaste, shampoo, soap, hairbrush, make up, make-up remover, creams
- 2 nightshirts. If you are planning to breast-feed, buy the ones with buttons down the front and think long in length rather than short. You may not want anything tight around your tummy straight after delivery.
- Socks – your feet may get cold in labour.
- Slippers, dressing gown, cardigan/jumper. If you have your baby in hospital think about what you will feel comfortable in as you may be in for a night or two.
- Disposable pants – 2 boxes of 6 minimum, for the first few days or extra large cheap cotton pants which may be more comfortable.
- Maternity pads – 2 boxes. They look like huge sanitary pads.

- Breast pads – 1 box for starters. Be prepared to change them regularly once your milk comes in. Some mothers have a lot of leakage from their nipples even when not feeding. There are many types of breast pads out there so if they don't feel comfortable, try different types.
- Optional extra – a small plastic jug – (*see* **Pelvic Care**).
- Clothes. Very few of you will get your shape back straight away and generally you will look about six months pregnant just after you have had your baby, so your pregnancy clothes will do.
- Plenty of change. In the hospital you pay for television and phone calls and it will not be cheap; also the hospital car park may be expensive.
- Camera (optional).
- Snacks – giving birth is hungry business. Your partner might want some too if it is a long labour! A straw may be useful if you need a drink while in labour.
- Book or magazine.

THE BASICS YOU NEED AT HOME

It can be a really exciting time preparing for your baby's arrival. Apart from getting your house in order so it is clean and safe (*see* **Baby-proofing your house**), other ideas that may help include freezing a few meals in advance, and stocking up on extra teabags and biscuits for any visitors.

Here are the essentials that you'll need:

Bedding

- Crib/cot/cot-bed. A lot will depend on how much money you want to spend. Cribs are small and can fit in your bedroom.
- Sheets: 3 minimum (one on, one in the wash or drying, one spare). If you have a baby who is often sick or possets, try placing a towelling square under its head so you can quickly change the square rather than a complete sheet every time. You will love this tip in the middle of the night when you are totally exhausted!
- Flat sheets (flannel): 3
- Baby sleeping bags: 2
- Cotton aerated blankets: 2 minimum

- Wool blanket for cold nights: 1 minimum
- Muslin cloths/squares

NB - Please read the medical section on **Cot death (SIDS)** before you go shopping for your bedding.

Baby kit

- **Newborn nappies** – you will need lots. Don't be surprised if your baby does a poo ten times in a day.
- **Nappy sacks** or bags – useful for hygiene and decreasing the smell.
- **Cotton wool balls** for topping and tailing (baby terminology for washing your baby, especially cleaning in between the skin creases).
- **Baby wipes**. Useful for everything from cleaning their bottoms to wiping their hand and faces when they start weaning. You know your child has grown up when you stop carrying them around with you wherever you go!
- **Non-biological washing powder** and a **germicidal non-biological pre-wash or soak**. (See **Washing baby's clothes**)
- **Sterilising equipment** if you are going to use bottles, although if you are only going to use a few you can just boil them in a large pan for five minutes then air-dry. (See **Bottles and sterilising**)
- **Support pillow**. These come in many different shapes and can be very useful during feeding. You place the support pillow on your lap then hold your baby on top and it helps take your baby's weight while you are feeding, relieving the pressure from your shoulders. If your baby is very small you may need an extra pillow to lift the baby up to the right height for you. You can also use the support pillow later on to support your baby when they are learning to sit up.
- **Newborn bibs** – very useful if you have a baby who possets.

Chairs

- **Pram/pushchair**. There are several things to bear in mind when choosing a set of wheels for your baby. If you are buying only a pushchair, make sure that the seat can lie flat; this is important for those early months when your baby is sleeping a lot and has poor head control. If you are tall, look for a pushchair with longer handles as pushing one around can put a lot of stress on your lower back. If you have a car, check that you can fit the pram/pushchair into its boot. If you will be using public transport then size and collapsibility are important. If you need a double buggy, make sure it can fit through an average door or shopping will be very difficult. The larger the wheels the easier it is to push over rough terrain.

- **Car seat**. There are many different shapes and sizes of car seats so make sure the car seat fits your car before you buy it. The shop assistants should be able to tell you or help you try the chair in your car before you buy it. NB - If there's an airbag in front of your baby's seat; make sure you deactivate it as they can cause suffocation.

- **Baby bouncing chair**. A great safe place to put your baby in while in the house. It should not be used all the time unless your baby has a lot of reflux; when they're awake, babies need to lie out flat and have a good kick and a play. This helps their physical development, especially strengthening their neck muscles. But a bouncing chair is useful until they can sit up on their own. NB - Never put a bouncing chair on a table as it can move when your baby wriggles or bounces.

2: YOUR BABY: Screening, Caring, Feeding, Sleeping, Crying, Washing

Caring for your baby can bring a total mixture of utter delight and happiness, but it can also feel overwhelming at times. Parenting is a skill that you learn, and it requires a lot of patience. Women do not turn into amazing mothers overnight, and men do not turn into amazing fathers overnight. Both of you are on a steep learning curve, so be kind to each other and know it is ok to make mistakes. If you are both devoted and talking about how to make life work for you and your baby or babies and children, it all helps and makes it easier and more fun.

Other parents and family will give advice and it is generally meant to be helpful but you can choose whether to use it or not. Do not compete with other parents and their babies because you have your personality and characteristics and your baby has theirs. Your baby will be able to walk and talk and be potty-trained eventually. Some babies will do things faster, other babies will take what seems like ages, but it is not a race – nor is it a sign of their intelligence. Every baby is different from the day they are born. The more energy, positive thinking and humour you can bring to it, the better your experience will be.

Newborn Screening

There are 3 screening processes one done by the doctor or midwife looking at the heart, hips, testes, cataracts and other anatomical abnormalities. The other carried out with a blood test. This is the heel prick test at age 5-8 days. It is checking for Phenylketonuria, hypothyroidism, Sickle Cell Disease, Thalassaemia, Cystic Fibrosis and MCAD deficiency. Finally there is a hearing test which is offered to all babies within 2 days in hospital or before 3 weeks old.

Vitamin K

Vitamin K deficiency causes a bleeding disorder. It is a rare disease but it is preventable by giving extra vitamin K after birth to all babies. It is given as a single injection.

Handling your baby

The more you handle your baby, the better you get. Generally, babies are happy to be held by anyone who is relaxed and confident. They only really form an opinion of who they want to be with when they are about 7 to 13 months old. To carry a newborn baby you need both arms – one to carry the body of your baby and the other to support the head. And when picking your baby up and out of the cot, support both the head and the bottom.

There are many different ways of holding your baby when they are very young. One way is to have your baby's face facing inwards, either with the head just above your chest or with the head just over your shoulder. Another method is to lay them over your forearm facing up or facing down. They like to lie facing down and have their backs rubbed, especially if they have colic.

Routine

Your own baby will have different needs from other people's babies – they don't all fit in to one mould. Some need lots of sleep, some need very little – just like adults. Try and work out when your baby wants to feed or sleep and see if there are any patterns in their timing; for example, your baby may want to sleep for two hours in the morning but not over lunchtime.

Consistency can help. Young children love to know what they are doing and are more relaxed when they know what is about to happen next, so they are happy to go to the same places all the time such as the park or the shops. The same goes for babies' feeds and sleeps. If they know they will feed and sleep, they do not worry about when the next meal is coming or become overtired. They will cry less, and on the odd day when life doesn't go according to plan, they will not cry endlessly when they are hungry. The same goes for sleep. If you put them in their cot the same way each day, they will learn to settle themselves (although some will take longer to learn this than others!). It also makes it easier for others to look after your baby if they know when your baby expects to feed and sleep. To make this happen they need to do roughly the same things each day.

If you get confused or cannot remember how many times you have fed your baby or how much sleep it has had, try making a note of feeding and sleeping times. But you do need to be flexible too. Your day will change when they have a growth spurt or become unwell and their needs for feeds or sleep change. All this is not easy when you are juggling lots of things. Then it is a balance of your new baby's needs and joining in with the family, so some give and take is needed.

A Rough Guide To The Number Of Feeds And Amount Of Sleep Babies Need Each Day

0-6 weeks Babies need about 6 to 8 feeds a day and about 16-18 hours' sleep a day. Some may need a lot less sleep. The other 6-8 hours will mainly be taken up with feeding. In the first few weeks they should not sleep for more than about 4 hours at one time. They will need regular naps throughout the day.

6 weeks to 5 months Babies need about five feeds a day. They need about 14-17 hours sleep a day – this will vary from child to child. Some of these hours of sleep will be naps during the day but most will hopefully be at night.

5-6 months They need about four feeds a day (some may still need five). During this time, if you are lucky, your baby can drop their night-time feed and sleep 12 hours at night, although not all are ready to do this. This is more likely if you are bottle-feeding, although breastfed babies can still sleep through. They will still need about two to four hours of sleep during the day.

6-12 months Once you have started weaning, your baby will end up with a minimum of three milk feeds a day (morning, afternoon and night) and three meals a day by the age of 12 months. Most will still need 2-4 hours of sleep during the day.

FEEDING

You can either breastfeed your baby or give them formula. Every baby is different. It is all about you enjoying your baby moment so do what is right for you.

Different ways to feed your baby

There are many different ways to feed and there is no true right way. Here are the main types:

• On demand: your baby tells you when he or she is hungry and off you go. You may end up with a lot of sleepless nights and a lot of feeds unless generally you naturally slip into your own feeding routine. Some of you will love this approach.

• Routine: if you follow a routine to the minute, your baby has to follow instructions and it is not easy if you are also trying to shop, cook, clean and even see a friend. It can also feel very demoralizing if you do not manage to keep up with the routine. However some of you may prefer to have this kind of structure to your day.

• Baby Friendly Hospital Initiative (BFI): encourages you to keep your baby close and respond to your baby's feeding cues. To feed whenever your baby wants to feed and for as long as your baby wants to feed. The aim of this baby-led feeding is to ensure a good milk supply and a contented baby. Your midwife will give you help and guidance with your breastfeeding.

• My way (which sort of includes all the methods above): a feed every 2-3½ hours and having a plan as far as possible in order to get all the feeds and sleeps in during the day to ensure you have a longer sleep at night, but with some flexibility. I know having some sleep is very important for me!

How often?

There is once again no right answer but I would advise as a rough guide to feed your baby **from the moment your baby is born, every 2-3½ hours – more often if recommended under medical supervision.**

Remember that at 0 to 6 weeks babies need about six to eight feeds in every 24 hours. Some babies are very sleepy and need to be woken up for each feed (*see* **The sleepy baby**). At night, stop feeding after about 10pm-11pm or thereabouts and see how long your baby sleeps before it wakes for the next feed. Hope for three to four hours' sleep; your baby should not go more than about four hours without a feed in the first few weeks due to the risk of hypoglycaemia which then causes them to be drowsy. (Hypoglycaemia is when there is not enough sugar in their body – never give sugar directly to your baby, give milk).

How much?

If you are breastfeeding and your baby is gaining weight with six to eight wet nappies a day, then do not worry how much milk your baby is getting at each feed. If your baby is possetting frequently then maybe review your breastfeeding (*see* **Possetting**). Some possetting is normal.

If you are bottle-feeding, as a rough guide, then the Department of Health has advised about 150ml-200ml (5oz-6.5oz) for each kg (2.2lb) of your baby's weight over 24 hours. For example if your baby weighed 3.18kg (7lb) that would be 477-636ml (16-21oz) a day in total. If you were giving 6 feeds a day then each feed would be about 80-106ml (2.6-3.5oz) a feed. The guidelines on the formula packets are another good source of information.

If your baby is losing weight, see your health visitor or your GP. (*See also* **Baby's weight**)

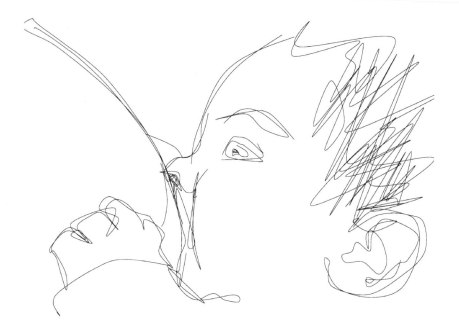

BREASTFEEDING

Some of you will find breastfeeding easier than others. If you can persevere for the first six weeks you have done well; six months is ideal, and anything over that is fantastic.

WHO (World Health Organisation) recommends that babies are breast-fed exclusively for the first six months. Breastfeeding provides excellent protection from infections and diseases. It also gives your baby's gut time to mature. There is also evidence that your baby will have better health, nutrition, higher intelligence and fewer allergies.

For those of you who can breastfeed once you get going you will become an expert. It can take a few weeks to get comfortable, so take one feed at a time. Some mothers produce more milk than others; breast size has nothing to do with it. Some of you will be overflowing and squirting out milk in all directions and others will just produce the minimum required. Bear in mind that breastfeeding can be very tiring and you will generally have more milk in the morning after some rest than in the evening. Breastfeeding does get easier after 6-12 weeks and the fullness and leaking also improves.

If your breast milk is decreasing in volume there are some medications which can be prescribed to increase milk production which you can discuss with your GP. This can be very helpful in the short term such as if you had been ill or suffered acute stress.

Getting started
Put your baby to your breast as soon as possible after birth but at least within six hours of birth. Medical emergencies may make this difficult but the staff will be able to help and advise you. The first breast milk you will produce is called colostrum, and it is yellow in colour. When the milk comes through on day three to five it starts to change, and by ten days, after your baby is born, you'll be producing breast milk that is more white and watery. The foremilk is grey and thin. The hind milk is thicker and more creamy-looking.

Some babies do not suck well for the first 2-3 days and live off their own reserves. Some babies need to recover from childbirth before they suck well. Skin to skin contact can help stimulate their hunger.

Where to breastfeed
Anywhere – some of you can! However some of you are uncomfortable with this and would rather be more discrete. You can choose clothes that are designed for simple access or a shawl over you and your baby. Try this in front of a mirror if you are unsure, to gain confidence. When out, ask if there is a mother's room, many shops and public places do offer them. Some places have a breastfeeding friendly sticker on the window. You could just make sure you are at home when you need to breastfeed – do what feels best for you not what others around you think you should be doing.

In position

Make yourself comfortable and well-supported. Sometimes a cushion behind your lower back can help to support it. Sit upright – a good posture helps to prevent back and shoulder pain. You can breastfeed lying down too which may be helpful if you have had a caesarean section.

One way to breastfeed is to have your baby across you (head higher than its stomach but not upright) with its head near your breast. You can put a lot of pillows on your lap or buy a semi-circular feeding/support cushion to raise your baby high enough on your lap to reach your breast without having to take your baby's weight on your upper back and shoulders.

Hold your baby so it has a straight back and is lying on its side, **so it does not have to turn its head to feed**. Use the arm nearest the breast you are about to feed from (left breast – left arm) to hold your baby's body and so that your baby's nose is the same height as your nipple. Then use your other hand to support the head. Take your baby to your breast, not the other way round. To encourage your baby to latch on, put your baby's lower lip to touch the underside of your nipple. Your baby should then open his or her mouth wide and take in the whole nipple area. Latching on is when your baby starts sucking. The suck reflex is stimulated when the nipple touches the top of your baby's mouth. Your baby's chin should touch your breast before its nose.

Correct position for suckling

Your nipple by now has turned a dark brown colour. The flat area around the nipple which is also dark brown is called the areola. The baby's mouth should have **the lower lip around most of the lower areola**, not just the nipple, and some of the upper lip should also cover the upper areola. Most of the sucking comes from the lower lip and lower jaw. When your baby feeds it breathes through its nose – so make sure their nose is not smothered by your breasts.

Also if your breasts are very engorged/full or if your milk comes in early sometimes expressing just a little – enough to soften the nipple – can help your baby get its mouth around to start feeding. Also, if your milk comes through fast and squirts out like fountains, expressing a little first can help your baby to feed comfortably and decrease the amount of possetting (*see* **Possetting**).

If your breast hurts or feels uncomfortable when your baby latches on then slide your finger into baby's mouth, release and start again. It is, however, not uncommon to experience a sharp pain when your baby first latches on (a few deep breaths can help) but the pain should subside in less than a minute and should not last the length of the feed. Once you get used to breastfeeding, it's very likely that you won't feel uncomfortable at all, and will just enjoy the feeling of closeness with your baby.

A good suckling position is needed for your baby to feed properly and gain weight. A poor suckling position can be a cause for your baby not to feed well and therefore not gain weight; it can also cause cracked nipples which are very painful. Just one painful feed could trigger cracked nipples (*see* **Breast Problems**).

Flat Nipples or Inverted Nipples
This can make breastfeeding very difficult and for some it may not be possible. Seek as much advice as you can. Nipple shields may help but not always.

Tongue Tie
Tongue tie is caused by a small piece of tissue that links the underside of your baby's tongue to the floor of the mouth. It can be a cause of poor feeding because your baby may not be able to attach on to your nipple or a bottle teat and then fail to get milk. Due to poor attachment your

nipples can become very cracked and sore and you are also at increased risk of mastitis (infection in your breast) as your breasts are not being drained of milk properly. You can look for it by lifting up your baby's tongue and comparing it to another baby who is feeding well. Your midwife is also trained to examine for tongue tie. It is treated at specialists units with a minor procedure to cut the tongue tie.

How long to breastfeed?

How long to let your baby feed for is a difficult question to answer. A feed in the very early days should be a maximum 20 minutes each time, especially if you want them to become good, efficient feeders. Once your baby has got the hang of breastfeeding it will feed for anything from ten minutes to an hour, although most will take between 20-40 minutes for each feed. It is important to distinguish feeding from comfort. One way to breastfeed is to think you are giving them a 'starter, main course and pudding' this encourages a really good feed on the first breast to get to all the hind milk. Then if your breast is completely empty and your baby is still hungry then offer the other breast.

Below is one way to start breastfeeding. You may follow it or just take ideas from it.

From birth to about day five after your baby is born

From the moment your baby is born and for the first five days or so, let them suckle for a maximum of ten minutes on each breast at each feed. That is both left and right breast equally at each feed. Your baby may only need five minutes each time on the first few days. Encourage your baby to have a little from both breasts. Then stop, and allow two to three and a half hours from the start of the last feed before giving the next feed. As mentioned above, stop at about 10pm–11pm and leave your baby to sleep, but for no more than about four hours, and see how you go.

If your baby wants to feed throughout the night then try and make them wait two hours each time. Always give your baby the night feeds but then work on encouraging the day feeds more. This encourages your baby to sleep longer at night and become an effective feeder rather than using your breasts as a comfort blanket. Do not let your baby suckle for long periods of time because you may get cracked nipples which are very painful.

This does work and you are not depriving your baby of anything as your milk only really comes through on day three to five. Before then there is only a small amount of colostrum present in your breast at any one time, so they don't need to be suckling for ages.

If your baby is crying (*see* **Crying**) all the time just after he or she is born it is not necessarily because they are hungry. Try wrapping them up tightly and holding them very close to you and saying 'ssh' repetitively – it can be amazingly calming and reassuring. When they are in a tight bundle it is similar to being inside your uterus/womb, and the 'ssh' noise is to imitate your blood going around your body, a familiar and comforting sound to your baby. Check if they need winding (*see* **Winding**) or if their nappy needs changing. If you are concerned about their crying, discuss this with your midwife or doctor.

The 'let down' reflex

When your milk comes through on day three to five, the milk collects behind the nipple ready for a feed and your breast becomes full. This is the 'let down'. True breast milk has generally arrived by day ten. You may leak or squirt milk from your nipples just before a feed so have your breast pads ready! Some of you will get a feeling of total relaxation when the milk comes in, others just get very thirsty, but for some of you it can cause painful uterine contractions, especially in the early days after birth.

Day five onwards

On about the fifth to the seventh day after giving birth, depending on the size of your baby (bigger babies may need to switch earlier), switch to one breast for ten to 40 minutes or so (your baby needs to empty that breast of milk) and then top up with the other side as needed – 'starter, main and desert'. Some babies are very fast feeders and may be finished in ten minutes, others may take longer. By the tenth day your milk has come in. This is made up of the fore milk (the first milk to come out, which is thirst-quenching) and the hind milk (the later thick calorific milk which is three times as rich as the fore milk and full of nutrition).

If your baby's nappy is very green then they are probably not getting enough hind milk. Hind milk is important for babies' development and growth. So it is important to empty the first breast fully – your baby needs to get to the thicker hind milk as it stays longer in the stomach, helping to fill baby up and put weight on. It is also important to empty the first breast fully to help avoid mastitis (*see* **Mastitis**). If your baby cannot make the two-hour space between feeds, then think about your milk quality and the amount of hind they are getting. The fore milk is very important for your baby's hydration. It is like giving a glass of water, and so is particularly important if it is hot.

After that keep going on the two- to three and a half-hourly feeds. **Always time feeds from the <u>start</u> (not the end) of your last feed, regardless of how long you were feeding.** Just as we all have body clocks and like to eat our meals at roughly the same time, so your baby will too.

If you want to feed your baby before it goes to sleep give your baby five minutes or so and take your baby off your nipple before your baby falls asleep.

Stop feeding after about 10pm to 11pm at night and see how long your baby sleeps for: hope for three to four hours, but four maximum in the first few weeks. Babies do wake up during the night because of their natural sleep cycle so they may just need to be settled again rather than fed each time. Sometimes delaying seeing them can give them the time to settle again without being disturbed.

Crying babies are not always asking for milk. Sometimes they just need a reassuring cuddle. Some babies do not get the idea of a full feed each time and can be hard to persuade, so you may have to increase the distractions between feeds to increase the times between feeds like taking them for a walk when they start to cry for food or play music or give them different toys to play with. Whatever works for your baby! Keep trying to get a structure of a feeding pattern with your baby. At the same time, remember they will have growth spurts (*see* **Growth spurts**) in which case they may need the extra feeds for a few days.

Which breast next?
Start on a different breast each time regardless of which one you finished on. Generally you start on the one you last used (the 'top up' side). If you don't your baby will not get the right balance of fore and hind milk and you may get different-sized breasts. There are many ways to remind yourself which breast you last fed from, such as a safety pin on your bra or moving your bracelet from one wrist to the other.

Breast milk
If your baby is not settling, especially at night, then look at your milk: it should look a rich creamy colour in general. If the milk is thin, watery and grey then it is probably not enough for your baby. To improve your breast milk, rest and eat well (*see* **What you should eat and drink**). If it doesn't improve and your baby is still not settling then add some milk formula. Try one feed a day – especially the evening or night feed. Be aware, though, that the top-up method – where you start with breastfeeding and then offer

formula in the bottle after – can work in the short-term but can sometimes stop your milk production as your baby doesn't take so much from the breast.

Try to **sleep or rest when your baby sleeps**. You can put them down to have a good kick near you and they can watch you cook or put a wash on – but you can't leave them awake while you sleep! So try to make your day fit around them and don't try and do lots of jobs when they are asleep or you will not get the rest you need.

Growth spurts

It is still not known how and when babies grow. However your baby will need to be fed more during each growth spurt. If you are breastfeeding, rest more (if possible), eat well and drink plenty of fluid during these phases. Your baby will demand more milk and your body will respond by making more at each feed over a few days. If you are bottle-feeding then go to the next level of feeds on the side of the packet. Your feeding pattern may change at this time and then after a few days it should all settle again. If your feeding pattern does not settle and your baby is crying all the time demanding lots of little feeds, you may need to distract your baby a little more in between feeds; try going for walks, using different toys or different noises. This should encourage them to have proper full regular feeds again.

The sleepy baby

NB: 0-6 week-olds need between six to eight feeds in 24 hours.

The sleepy baby is a well baby who just needs a bit of encouragement to feed. Some of you do not like to wake a sleeping baby. This is very natural but if your baby sleeps through the day it will need to feed at night. If you want to get your baby feeding through the day you may have to **wake your baby up to breastfeed or bottle feed**. In the first few weeks babies sleep about 16 hours a day, so you only have eight hours left to get six to eight feeds in. It is important to feed regularly in the early days to avoid hypoglycaemia (not enough sugar in the body as mentioned earlier) or jaundice. After about the third to fourth week they tend to be less sleepy. You may need to wake your baby during the night to get the feeds in too.

Make sure your baby is **properly awake** before you start feeding. Think first about the room temperature: babies prefer a warm environment to a hot one – about 16-20°C. Any hotter and they may become very drowsy while feeding. Try taking off a layer of their clothing; you may need to strip them down to their nappy provided it is not too cold. Alternatively turn down the heating or open a window. Rubbing your baby's toes, talking to them or singing may also help wake them up. Skin to skin contact can help stimulate hunger. Spend the time waking them up, especially during the day, or you will miss a feed which will mean that you have to get up again at night.

Once they are feeding they may stay latched on, but stop sucking. This is normal as babies feed in cycles of fast sucking, then slow sucking then pausing before starting off again. They may be waiting for the next milk to arrive, they may need winding or they may have lost interest. To encourage them to suck again try stroking their skin just in front of their ear. Alternatively 'compress' or squeeze your breast to encourage the milk out to help speed up the flow of milk to keep them interested.

Breast refusal
Babies can often refuse your breast. This can come and go so stay calm. Check your baby is well. Do not worry if they miss a feed. At 3-5 months babies can become easily distracted so they may need a really quiet place to feed each time. This is not always easy to manage. Other causes may be thrush either in their mouth or your breast (*see* **Breast Problems**), teething or being unwell. The taste

of your breast-milk can change with antibiotics, the time of your monthly cycle, nipple creams, perfumes and what you eat. If they have a dummy the sucking action is different and your baby may prefer the dummy.

Expressing milk

You can start expressing milk from day one but most start at about two weeks onwards unless there is a medical reason. Many breastfeeding mothers don't feel the need to. But for some, expressing will help maintain effective breastfeeding as well as enabling someone else to feed your baby with your milk. Expressing increases the demand for milk, so when your baby has a growth spurt you'll have enough to cope with the increased demand. When you've got the hang of it all, try expressing milk during the day so that your partner can feed the baby in the evening while you get some extra sleep. Working mothers may find expressing a helpful aid to maintaining breast milk supply. NB - Expressing milk increases your supply, so if you are already producing a lot of breast milk, even a little bit of milk expressed may increase your supply significantly.

There are three ways to express milk, at the start it may seem a lot of effort for not a lot and you do feel like a cow being milked!

- **By hand**. Massaging your breasts will produce a little milk unless you are naturally producing a lot of milk – a hot bath may help.
- **Using a hand pump**. The hand-held pump works if you can naturally produce a lot of milk.
- **The electric express breast pump** does work well. There are either large hospital express pumps or mini ones available from shops and pharmacies. The mini-express pumps are very effective and much cheaper but not as good as the larger ones.

To help increase your milk supply you **only need to express after about two feeds a day**. Try for five minutes to start with and increase to ten minutes after doing it for a week or so and see how much extra milk you can take off. If it completely stresses you out then don't do it. It is meant to be an aid and it is not essential.

Expressed milk can be placed in a sterilised bottle or specially designed freezer bottles. Alternatively, use sterilised ice cube trays, then take the cubes out and store in sealed bags in the freezer. (To sterilise an ice cube tray, clean well then submerse in water and boil it for 10 minutes). Always label and date the expressed milk. It can be kept in the fridge at 4°C (the back of the fridge, not the door) for up to five days, or stored in the ice compartment of a fridge for two weeks or in the freezer for up to six months. Do not re-freeze it once it has been thawed.

To defrost the milk, ideally take it out in advance and let it defrost in the fridge. Placing it in a pan and gently heating it or placing it in a bottle warmer will speed the process up. Defrosting in a microwave is not recommended but best saved for emergencies.

Milk can be given cold from the fridge, room temperature or warm. Some babies have a strong opinion so try different temperatures. Always check the temperature by dripping some on your wrist before giving the milk to your baby.

What you should eat and drink
When you breastfeed everything you eat and drink is shared with your baby. So drink plenty of fluids – a large glass of water every time you breastfeed. (See **Alcohol and breastfeeding**) Eat as much home-cooked food as possible and avoid processed food if possible.

Breastfeeding uses an extra 500 calories a day. Some of this is taken from the fat stores laid down during pregnancy. A few of you may not have many fat stores so you will need to eat more. If you are hungry eat lots of fruit, vegetables and fibre – go for the healthy snack. This helps keep your blood sugar levels even and also balances your emotions as it stops the sugar highs and lows. A lot of refined sugar or chocolate will only give you a moment of energy followed by a feeling of tiredness. Try and think of healthy snacks or distracting yourself... though that's easier said than done!

In my experience, some mothers struggle with breastfeeding because they are not eating enough. I have found that the situation generally improves if they eat three good meals a day, and some needed healthy snacks in between, too.

Some foods such as lettuce, cabbage, onions and some beans can upset your baby – so look at the nappies and be aware that what you eat may be irritating your baby. Also (*see* **Colic**). Your baby may have a dairy intolerance and have smelly odd poo and/or dry skin or eczema; taking dairy out of your diet for two weeks may help. If that makes no difference, then start eating it again.

It is best for you and your baby to have a well-balanced healthy diet. However, if you are very grey-eyed and tired, it might be a good idea to have an iron and vitamin D level blood test by your GP. When you take a supplement, check it is suitable for breastfeeding. The importance of vitamin D in pregnancy and breastfeeding has only been noticed relatively recently; hence all the advice, and in general you are recommended to take a vitamin D supplement every day.

Nicotine, Caffeine, Drugs and Breastfeeding
Nicotine (smoking), caffeine and drugs (prescribed, over the counter or illegal) can all affect your baby's feeding, sleeping and digestion.

Smoking Cigarettes
A lot of research has been done on smoking cigarettes and breastfeeding. Babies consume more nicotine from the air

around them than from breast milk. Smoking and breastfeeding may have a direct effect on your baby, causing colic, increased crying, restless sleep, nausea, vomiting, diarrhoea and abdominal cramps. Your baby has major brain growth in its first year and smoking can affect your baby's brain development in the long term.

If you are going to continue smoking and breastfeeding it is recommended that you smoke after a feed so your body has time to clear the nicotine before the next feed. Your body contains the highest concentration of cigarette smoke while you are smoking. It takes between 90 minutes to 2 hours for the nicotine levels from one cigarette to halve in your body, and about 72 hours from the last cigarette to clear your body of nicotine completely. The more you smoke in a day, the stronger the effect of the nicotine. Research has shown that the nicotine in cigarettes blocks the effects of prolactin (a hormone needed for breastfeeding), causing less breast milk to be made. If you smoke just before a feed it also affects the 'let down reflex' and so less milk is released.

It is believed, however, that if you are going to continue to smoke then it is better to breastfeed than use formula, as breast milk does provide some protection against the effects of the nicotine as well as all the positives that it provides normally.

'Second-hand' smoke – that is, smoke from people smoking in the same room – also affects your baby. Babies brought up in a smoky environment commonly have an increase in respiratory problems, such as chest infections or croup, ear infections, allergies and also Cot Death (*See* **Cot death**). So if you are going to smoke then it is recommended to smoke in another room or, more ideally, outside and away from your baby. After your cigarette, change your clothes, wash your hands and rinse out your mouth before handling your baby again as the nicotine also clings to your clothes and saliva.

Do not smoke in your car with your baby.

Ideally you are recommended to stop smoking when breastfeeding. Nicotine is highly addictive and stopping is not easy. If you want to try to stop then going 'cold turkey' is the best way but not necessarily the easiest. Nicotine patches are not necessarily recommended as they provide a continuous stream of nicotine into the breast milk. Other types of nicotine substitutes such as gums, lozenges, microtabs or inhalers are better as they are taken intermittently, so you can take your breastfeeding times into consideration. Smoking also decreases your absorption of vitamin C, so taking a supplement will help.

Caffeine
There is no exact research on the amount of caffeine you should have in a day while breastfeeding, but two mugs of instant coffee or tea or one mug of filter coffee seems to be about the recommended amount. Remember caffeine is also in some fizzy drinks and chocolate.

Drugs
Please check with your pharmacist or doctor before you take ANY medicines while you are breastfeeding whether they are prescribed, over the counter or alternative.

Illegal drugs all affect your baby so stopping is strongly recommended. Breastfeeding while taking cocaine, heroin or PCP is not safe for your baby due to addiction and even death. Marijuana and breastfeeding can cause sedation, weakness and growth delays in your baby along side all the effects of smoking cigarettes. There is a lot of help out there if you ask for it and follow the advice given, however hard it is for you.

www.nhs.uk smoking or illegal drugs
www.patient.co.uk or NHS smoking helpline 0800 022 4332, open 7 days a week, 7am-11pm.

Alcohol and breastfeeding

Remember that everything you consume goes to your baby. Alcohol passes into breast milk which can affect your baby's feeding, sleeping and digestion. Research has shown that alcohol also affects the production of breast milk. It decreases the oxytocin levels which causes the 'let down reflex' to slow down so it takes longer to release the milk. Alcohol also increases the prolactin levels so mothers have a feeling of fullness; you think you have lots of milk but you actually have less than you realise so your baby may still be hungry. However a small amount of alcohol in the breast milk will not do your baby any long-term harm.

Alcohol is not 'trapped' in breast milk, so it will decrease in its concentration over time. Alcohol clears from your blood at about the rate of one unit every two hours. One unit is half a pint of 3.5% beer or one small glass (125ml) of wine. It is best to drink alcohol after breastfeeding, not before. No one knows the exact safe amount of alcohol you can drink but a guide of one to two units, once or twice a week would be good to follow.

Alternatively, if there is a special occasion and you get a little carried away, use milk that you expressed before the event, and express and discard any breast milk from during and after the occasion.

If you get very severe hangovers or feel unwell after a glass of alcohol, then avoid alcohol until you have stopped breastfeeding. Make sure you drink plenty of water at the same time as drinking alcohol as it is very easy to become dehydrated when breastfeeding. Bear in mind you will also have to get up during the night for your baby and you won't be getting the recovery time you used to have after a night out!

For more information on alcohol especially on units of alcohol *see* www.drinking.nhs.uk

How to stop breastfeeding

Do not stop breastfeeding suddenly – drop one feed at a time. Some advise dropping a feed a week, but that depends on you and your breasts. I recommend you drop one feed at a time and wait until, at that time of day, your breasts stop becoming engorged; for the first few days you may need to express a little at this time to make your breasts more comfortable. Watch out for mastitis (see **Mastitis**) at this time and keep massaging the blocked areas. Do not rush stopping – try and plan it.

If you want to switch your baby over to bottles at some point before they are one year old, for example if you are planning to go back to work, then introduce a bottle early just for one feed a day. It is best to do this by the end of the first month, because by the third month they will have a very strong opinion that breast is best!

The best time to introduce them to the bottle is the late-evening feed – you can express earlier that day and then give the bottle to your partner and go to bed early.

If your baby has never had formula and you want to stop breastfeeding, they may like the new formula milk. If they do not like the formula, try mixing breast milk and formula. Another technique for swapping over is to start on the breast and then swap to the bottle – have the teat very near and hope their hunger drives them to keep sucking and they don't realise and just get on with it. You could even have breast milk in the bottle so the taste does not change.

The worse-case scenario is suddenly deciding to change to bottle and your baby not liking it so refusing to take its milk – some can be very stubborn and take up to 24 hours to change! So try and start early if you can.

Alternatively, you can exclusively breastfeed and go straight onto a cup/beaker/open egg-cup. Try and find someone else to give the cup of milk and be out of the room, as your smell and your baby's expectations will not help.

You can always ask your midwife, health visitor or local lactation consultant for advice. Alternatively, contact the breastfeeding helplines:

National Breastfeeding Helpline:
www.nationalbreastfeedinghelpline.org.uk

Association of Breastfeeding Mothers:
www.abm.me.uk 08444 122949

The Breastfeeding Network:
www.breastfeedingnetwork.org.uk 0300 1000212

La Leche League www.laleche.org.uk 08451 202918

National Childbirth Trust www.nct.org.uk 08704 448708

The Breastfeeding Network – with breastfeeding support in Bengali and Sylhetti 0300 4562421

NON-BREASTFEEDING MUMS

If you decided to bottle-feed straight away, your breasts will still become engorged with milk between the days two to seven after your baby is born. This can be very painful but it will not last long. Ice packs and squeezing a little milk at this time can help. Hot baths and showers however stimulate milk production so are best avoided. The worse of the engorgement should pass in 12-48 hours, although occasional leaking may occur for a few weeks after.

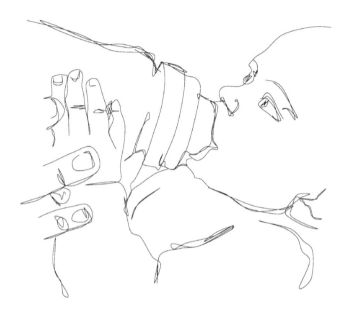

BOTTLE FEEDING

You will need:

- About six to eight bottles
- Teats to go with the bottles
- A bottle and teat brush
- A steriliser – either boiling water, sterilising tablets or a steriliser (electric or microwave type).

Sterilising

It is important to sterilise your baby's bottles for the first six to 12 months. Do not stop before six months and continue after that for as long as you feel comfortable. After six months your baby will be putting things in its mouth and you cannot watch them all the time, especially outside on the grass or on the beach. I have heard it called 'good clean dirt! There is also a lot of evidence that a little dirt is good for a baby's immune system and means they are less likely to get asthma and allergies.

To sterilise you need to be meticulous. Buy a good steriliser. Some are electric and others work in the microwave. The alternative is a disinfectant tablet placed in a container of water for 30 minutes and left to soak, or placing the bottles in boiling water for 10 minutes. If you use a disinfectant then rinse the bottles with cooled boiled water not tap water.

To sterilise bottles: take the bottles apart; the teat is separate from the white ring. Wash them in soapy water and rinse well, or put through the dishwasher and check they are clean. Then place in the steriliser, add the required amount of water and switch on. When the steriliser has finished leave to cool as they are very hot at first, but take out before two hours or the bottles will no longer be sterilised. Put the bottles back together; either hold the teat by the edge or use the white U-shaped piece of plastic to put the teat in place so you do not touch it.

There are many different teats. They are labelled according to the age of your baby so the speed the milk that comes out varies. They come in all shapes and sizes. Different babies like different shaped teats.

Formula milk
There are many different brands of formula milk and stages of formula. Start with stage 1 or First Infant Formula until your baby is at least 6 months old and follow the advice on the side of the packaging. The majority are based on cow's milk, which should be your first choice. Do not give your baby soya milk formula, goats milk formula or any other form of milk unless under medical supervision. If you need dairy-free formula milk there are two types. One is based on cow's milk that has had the lactose removed so are lactose free (LF). The other type is specially designed fully hydrolysed protein formula milk for the baby who is allergic to cow's milk protein. There are other formulas designed for premature and low birth weight babies to help catch up.

How often and when to start are the same for breastfeeding and there is no right answer but as a rough guide feed your baby **from the moment your baby is born, every 2-3½ hours – more often if under medical supervision.** Continue until about 10pm–11pm and then leave your baby to sleep, but for no more than about four hours in the first few weeks, and see how you go. Some babies will be easier than others!

Follow the recommendations on the side of the packet and try not to over-or under-feed your child (*also see* **How Much**). As a rough guide if you are bottle-feeding then the Department of Health has advised about 150ml-200ml (5oz-6.5oz) for each kg (2.2lb) of your baby's weight over 24 hours. For example if your baby weighed 3.18kg (7lb) that would be 477-636ml (16-21oz) a day in total. If you were giving 6 feeds a day then each feed would be about 80-106ml (2.6-3.5oz) a feed. Your baby's age or weight is a good indicator.

If it is a hot day, or your baby is a bit constipated, you can always try giving cooled boiled water on its own, or adding an extra 30mls (1oz) of water to the bottle feed.

If your baby seems particularly hungry after 6 months you can try hungry baby formula, there is however very little evidence for this, it is not recommended before 6 months.

If your baby is hungry before 6 months then you could increase the size of feeds or number of feeds a day within reason. Once you have finished the feed if your baby wants more try distracting your baby.

It is better your baby learns to eat what it needs rather than eating as much as he or she can before feeling full. Also discuss this with your health visitor.

To make a formula bottle

Powdered formula is not sterile but the ready-to-feed liquid formula is sterile. The Department of Health (DOH) has a gold standard method based on the evidence of very rare bacteria that live in the powdered formula that can make your baby ill. These bacteria will be killed in water above 70°C. Firstly you need to sterilise the bottles (*see* **Sterilisation**). Next, you need to fill the bottle with hot *'once-boiled'* water. This means emptying the kettle completely, refilling with tap water and boiling once only, and using within 30 minutes. Please note: bottled water may contain too much salt (too much salt (Na) is over 200mg/L and too much sulphate (SO or SO_4) is 250ml/L - see the side of the bottle). **Note:** *un-boiled bottled water is **not** sterile water*. Once-boiled water contains less salt than twice-boiled water, and is better for your baby's kidneys. Fill the bottle with this water to the required amount and then add the formula. A scoop is a **levelled-off** scoop-full, not heaped and do not add extra scoops. Shake and then cool under a tap to about room temperature. Before you give any heated milk, check the temperature by dripping some on the inside of your wrist; this is a very sensitive area (your palm is not as sensitive).

This takes time so it will make life easier if you are organised and get all the bottles sterilised together in advance; otherwise you'll have a baby crying for its bottle, and that is stressful. Leave the sterilised bottles out on the side in your kitchen or in the fridge. The sterilised bottles need to be used within 24 hours.

This method may not be that easy to follow with day to day living. You could add the formula to a little boiled water to dissolve and then add pre-cooled boiled water kept in a sterilised bottle to cool it quickly. Check the temperature.

You can make up the feeds in advance and store in the fridge for 24 hours then warm up the feeds to serve either in hot water or a bottle warmer. Microwaves are not recommended due to the uneven heating of the formula milk so some of the formula milk can be very hot and may burn your baby's mouth.

- Once cooled in the fridge for about an hour you can keep the pre-made formula in a cool bag with an ice-pack for 4 hours.
- Formula that has been made up and kept at room temperature has to be consumed or thrown away within 2 hours.
- Ready-to-feed liquid infant formula once opened can be stored in the fridge for up to 24 hours. This is already sterile and can be very useful if out and about.

Baby's weight

If your baby's weight is not following the expected weight line (centile) then seek medical care.

Your baby should weigh more than its birth-weight at 4 weeks. Regular weight checks are the best way to monitor the progress of your baby. Plot the weights in the weight chart in the red book that you are given when your baby is born. Ask your health visitor for guidance if you are unsure.

If your baby's weight stays the same or your baby loses weight, see your health visitor or doctor. If you are breastfeeding sometimes it can be simply a matter of eating more and resting more.

If your baby is gaining too much weight then think about how much you are feeding them. It is very hard to over-feed a breastfed baby. Follow the guidelines on the side of the packet for formula feeding. If you or your husband is particularly tall then maybe you have a large baby, but seek advice.

Do not give your baby anything other than milk (or water) for the first six months. You can start weaning after 4 months but the advice is to start at about 6 months. Do not give your baby any sweets or chocolate until at least six months (two years ideally). Apart from tooth decay, which starts very early on, once your child has had sugary foods/sweets/refined sugar they may become fussier eaters, preferring biscuits to broccoli.

Vitamins ACD for your baby

The Department of Health recommends that normal term babies from 6 months onwards that are breastfed should be given vitamins ACD, and formula-fed babies should start when they are having less than 500mls of infant formula a day until aged 5 years. The vitamins can be bought over the counter unless you are entitled to free vitamins from 'Healthy Start' via your health visitor. You can give too many vitamins, so choose only one supplement at any one time.

POSSETTING

Possetting is when your baby brings up some of its feed either when burping or just after a feed, and it is very common. Sometimes this may be a lot of milk, and it may seem that they are not taking any in. It often looks like more than it actually is. A weekly weight check will monitor it; if your baby is gaining weight, don't worry and keep going. If they are losing or not gaining weight then seek medical advice.

If you are breastfeeding you may be giving them too much milk at each feed; try feeding them for less time at each feed. If you produce a lot of milk try to express a few mls first before starting each feed. Remember that the foremilk is as important as the hind so you still have to try to give a bit of both, but if they are possetting a lot they may not be getting enough hind milk. If you are bottle-feeding and your baby seems to posset after certain feeds, then try giving them less at those feeds. If a smaller feed helps them, work out how to get an extra feed in during the day. Keep your baby upright after each feed and avoid too-vigorous winding.

If your baby is possetting after every meal, he or she may have both a weak valve and muscles at the top opening of the stomach so food naturally flows up rather than downwards or reflux (*see* **reflux**). Your doctor can advise on medicines which can be very effective. If they start to vomit with force or more frequently, please consult medical advice.

WINDING
Babies need winding after every feed. As your baby gets older it will need less winding. Always wind after every feed when your baby is first born then reassess if it is needed as your baby gets older. Sometimes your baby will need winding in the middle of a feed.

There are many different ways to wind:

One way is to sit your baby on your lap, well supported, or along your forearm or over your shoulder and rub its back in a rotational manner. Sometimes gentle patting on the back will help. Another way is to sit your baby upright on your lap and gently lift him or her up with your hands under their arms. This may not be appropriate for very young babies as you may not be able to hold their head at the same time.

My favourite way is to listen for the 'bubbles' in their tummy first by putting my ear to their tummy and listening. The 'bubbles' sound just like water 'sloshing' inside a balloon. Then sit your baby on your lap and hold your baby under the arms but with your fingers supporting their head and gently rotating/twisting their upper body just enough to move the fluid inside their tummy around. Then keep rotating/twisting one way and then the other until the 'wind' centrifuges/spins up. Keep going until all the bubbles have gone.

When you bottle-feed, watch the bottle and make sure the milk is always covering the teat; if not, your baby will suck in air which means they will need more winding. Most babies like to be upright for a few minutes after a feed which is normal but if they cry after every feed and won't be laid down flat, consider reflux (*see* **reflux**) and see your GP.

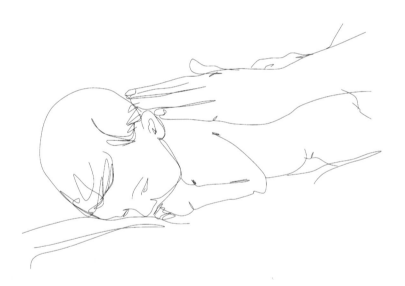

COLIC

Colic is when your baby is drawing up its knees, arching backward, crying, clenching its fists and looking distressed. Their tummies are often very hard at the time. It is presently a name for a variety of symptoms that cause your baby to be in distress and cry, but as yet no one has proved what colic really is. It often occurs in the afternoon.

It generally starts aged about two weeks, is worse at six weeks and mostly has cleared up by three months. Your baby continues to gain weight and thrive during this time and, when not crying, is perfectly normal.

If your baby has fed every two to three and a half hours or so from the day they are born, in my experience they seem to suffer less. Think how you feel on Christmas Day when you have been eating food on and off all day with no real break in between meals: by 4-5pm your stomach feels over-full, you feel out of sorts and have to sit down for a while. Well, being fed a little bit here and a little bit again throughout the day may have a similar effect on your baby's stomach and they too feel uncomfortable. So I encourage you to give your baby's stomach a break between feeds. Smaller babies may need more frequent feeds, especially if your baby is a premature baby or under special instructions.

REDUCING COLIC
Breastfeeding
If you are breastfeeding you may be giving your baby too much foremilk and not enough hind. To increase the amount of hind milk you give to your baby, try putting your baby back on your breast for a further feed to encourage a longer feed each time. If they usually feed for 20 to 30-minute feeds they may still need longer on that breast before you top up with the other side. Alternatively express some milk before you start feeding so you increase the amount of hind they take. The fore milk is still necessary for their hydration.

Diet
If you are breastfeeding, think carefully about what you are eating as some babies can be sensitive to your diet. Some of the foods to be wary of are: lettuce, cabbage, green beans, broccoli, onions, strawberries, grapes, cranberries, citrus fruits, spicy food/chilli, garlic, nuts, chocolate, caffeine (coffee in particular) and alcohol.

Cow's milk in your diet can also irritate your baby's stomach. To test if a particular food affects your baby you have to take it out of your diet completely for two weeks, then reintroduce it and wait for three days. If there is no change then start eating that food again and try something different. If the symptoms return, avoid that food until you stop breastfeeding. Some mums find drinking chamomile tea helps although there is very little scientific evidence to support this.

Bottle-feeding
If your baby is bottle-fed, changing the type of bottle may help. Some bottles are designed for babies with colic; ask your pharmacist if unsure. Or try a different type of formula: if another standard formula makes no difference, try one that's lactose-free. If lactose–free formula helps then use it for a few weeks then try to re-introduce standard formula again. Every time you initiate a change, continue that change for a few days – ideally for a week – to see if things improve. A one-off change in formula may not give the body enough time to recover and change. If your baby is instantly worse on a new formula, however, stop straight away and go back to the previous formula or try another one.

Colic remedies from your pharmacy may help.

Other ways to help with colic which are not supported by research but parents have found helpful include:

• Rubbing their tummy may help – always in a clockwise direction. Baby oil mixed with a couple of drops of lavender is also very soothing when rubbed on their tummy. Laying them on your forearm, facing downwards, and rubbing their back is also soothing.

• Warm up their tummies with a warm towel or a warm hot water bottle wrapped in a towel (be very careful not to burn).

• Baby massage which can be very helpful. If there isn't a baby massage course available near you, you could try reading a book and trying to follow the instructions. Your midwife may be able to give you further advice.

• Sometimes distraction with various noises works; often a repetitive noise is effective such as a washing machine, vacuum cleaner or a drive in a car.

• Craniosacral osteopathy can be very good for colic. Make sure the craniosacral osteopath is registered; you can always ask around other mothers or your health visitor for recommendations.

• A teaspoon of mildly warmed chamomile tea after each feed may help. Other alternative ideas include fennel, liquorice root or catnip. None of these are scientifically proven.

• Homeopathy may help.

If your baby still has colic then see your health visitor or doctor. It may be reflux (*see* **Reflux**) and respond to medical treatment.

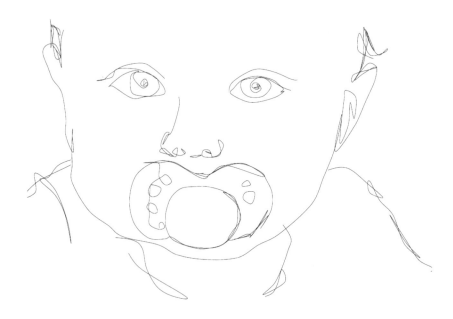

Dummies

Dummies are not recommended until breastfeeding has been established (at least one month).

Dummies can help comfort some babies and settle them to sleep; others might suck their thumbs. If they are a 'sucky' baby then they will like one or the other. The advantage of a dummy is that you can get rid of it when they get older; but at least a thumb-sucker will not wake you up at night when they can't find their dummy! There is current evidence that a dummy can reduce cot deaths if used to settle for each sleep once breast feeding is established.

The effect on their teeth depends on how they suck and how they use their tongue to push on their teeth. This is hard to predict, but if you can persuade your child to stop either their thumb or dummy before the adult teeth come in at six years old then it should not make much difference to their teeth long-term. Ideally a dummy should be stopped between 6 and 12 months.

Babies do not need the dummy in their mouth all the time. If they do have the dummy all the time it may become even harder to stop. Do not coat the dummy in anything sweet or it will rot their teeth when they are older.

Always sterilise the dummy when your baby is very young in particular. Cleaning a dummy in your own mouth is not the same as sterilising.

Try to avoid ribbons or strings attached to the dummy as they can get caught around their neck.

Hiccups

It is common, and normal, for your baby to hiccup after a feed; your baby will even have been hiccuping in your tummy from time to time. Put them down to sleep as usual – they are fine. Baby massage can help hiccups. I have also found that bottle- or breastfeeding your baby tilted gently downwards (rather than being upright) can help, even though it may seem odd. If your baby gets upset by the hiccups then seek advice.

WEANING

The ideal time to wean your baby – start introducing them to solid foods – is when they are four to six months old. There is still a lot of debate about when to start weaning and there is no right answer. If your baby is waking up at night hungry then if you are breastfeeding try adding another feed or change one of the feeds to formula. If you are bottle feeding then sometimes another feed is needed or some cooled boiled water. Or start weaning. Every baby is different so a bit of trial and error is needed.

Some key things to remember are:

- Never leave your baby alone with food.
- It should be a fun experience – not a battle.
- Try not to attach your emotions to food.
- Avoid getting angry or worried if they do not eat anything.
- It is about trying foods rather than how much.
- Food needs to be explored.

- If your child realises that they get your attention more by not eating, they may decide to take their time.
- At the end of the meal check their mouths to see if it is empty – ask them to 'open-wide', some babies can store food in their cheeks.

Your baby needs to be able to sit upright so the food can to be moved around the mouth to be swallowed. The food will then be mixed with saliva which will increase absorption of the nutrients. Some babies like a spoon others want to do it all by themselves and think self-feeding is more fun.

When you first start out weaning, it is more to get your baby used to different textures in its mouth than for the nutritional value of the food, so do not worry about volume. Weaning with just pureed food can make it harder to introduce lumpy foods so let them try some finger foods early on. They still get most of their nutrition from milk to begin with, though this gradually reduces by the time they are 8-12 months. If they love food, then watch out for excessive weight gain: your baby may need less milk. Also watch out for your baby not drinking enough because he or she is full up with food. The small amounts of food you give them needs to be high in nutritional value – they need a lot of vitamins and minerals to grow.

There are many different theories on weaning from pureed food to baby–led weaning and there is no right answer. So long as you are happy and your baby is relaxed with a few simple rules it should not be stressful.

Keep the food simple to start with. Baby rice, vegetables and a little fruit are the basics. Start with very small amounts (about 1 to 2 teaspoons full or pieces) and build up. To make the texture soft, strain, puree or mash the food and add a little breast or formula milk. Introduce different foods slowly with only a few sweeter foods at first. Once you get started try to offer as much variety as possible.

If you end up weaning before 6 months then there is some research to suggest that some foods may cause allergies if given too early and so should be <u>avoided until at least 6 months</u>. The foods that have been linked to these allergies are wheat-based foods e.g. bread, rusks, some breakfast cereals and also eggs, nuts, seeds, fish, shellfish and unpasteurised cheeses. This theory and list could change at any time! The advice on wheat changes all the time – there are a lot of unknowns! Also see **What Food When and Why?**

Below are some vegetables and fruits to try:

Steamed, roasted, stir-fried or lightly boiled vegetables – any of them such as: carrots, peas, swede, parsnips, green beans, broccoli, baby sweet corn, cauliflower, sweet potato, courgette, pumpkin, aubergine, potato, peppers, yam, mushroom.

Avocado, sticks of cucumber (great if teething), tomato

Fruit: Pear, apple, banana, pear, orange, peach, nectarine, mango, prunes in their own juice not syrup, apricot, berries, watermelon

Other ideas for foods to start adding for variety:

Baby rice, breadsticks, rice cakes, toast fingers, oats, unsweetened breakfast cereals, pasta, chapatti fingers, pitta bread

Meat – lamb, beef, chicken, duck, turkey, fish
Lentils, pulses and beans
Egg, cheese, yoghurt

SIMPLE RULES TO FOLLOW

WHAT FOOD WHEN AND WHY?

Apr

- **Protein** should not be given before six months of age and ideally from seven to eight months onwards. This gives your baby's stomach a chance to learn to digest easy food first. Meat can be very difficult to swallow and may initially need blending.

- **Dairy foods** can be introduced in cooking from six months onwards but it is recommended to use formula rather than cow's milk in the bottle feeds until your child is one year old. Use full-fat milk until they are at least two years old as they need the fat for vitamin absorption and brain development. If your baby is over-weight semi-skimmed milk may be recommended but you also need to be looking at the other foods you are giving your baby.

2/ Feb

- No **goat's milk**, **sheep's milk** or **oat milk** until 1 year old.

- No **rice milk** until 5 years old.

- **Wheat** should be included it in their diet unless there is a medical reason or family history of coeliac or intolerance to wheat in which case add it in after a year old. (Advice on wheat is still changing.)

- **Eggs** can cause allergies and it is generally recommended to start cooking eggs well from eight months onwards.

May

- **No honey** until a year old as it can contain a bacteria which can harm babies.

- **Nuts** can cause allergies and the advice is very mixed at present. If you have a nut allergy in the family or hay fever, severe eczema or severe allergic asthma, then avoid until three years old. Otherwise it is safe to introduce ground nuts from six months onwards. Do not give whole nuts to children until they are five years old as there are still a few children who choke to death on foods such as peanuts every year.

- **Fish** are very nutritious but can also cause allergies. Try any of the oily fish such as salmon, tuna, mackerel or white fish such as cod, haddock or plaice from 6 months onwards. Look out for the fish bones. Shellfish should not be introduced until after 12-18 months.

- **Cut up all fruit** such as cut grapes in half when they can eat finger foods by themselves. Remove all stones from fruit such as plums and cherries until they are five years old.

- **Remove skin from all food** when they first start weaning, e.g. sausages. Peel apples and pears.

- Babies should not be on a high-fibre diet such as bran as it fills them up and stops them eating what they really need.

- They need **good fats** such as oily fish, vegetable oils, olive oil, oils in nuts and seeds, cheese and yoghurt for brain development. Avoid 'bad' fats such as hydrogenated fats and trans-fatty acids which are found in biscuits, crisps, chocolates, some ready-made meals and some margarine.

- **Do not add salt** to food because your baby's kidneys have not fully developed until they are at least two years old. You may not like the taste of their food but you do not have to eat it! If buying ready-made baby food, check for both sugar and salt content. Buy unsalted butter. Do not use stock cubes as they often contain a lot of salt.

- **Avoid sugar** when you start weaning as it can stop them eating the healthy foods and cause tooth decay even though your baby has no teeth when it starts weaning. Sugar is hidden in lots of foods – look out for words like: sucrose, dextrose, fructose, glucose and corn syrup, aspartamine. Molasses is a great, very nutritious, natural sweetener but use sparingly.

- **Offer water** with each meal, if you want to give fruit juice then dilute it 1-10 and offer only at meal time, to prevent tooth decay. Water has to be cooled boiled water for under 6 month olds, otherwise use tap water.

Never give fizzy drinks or squash to babies or toddlers.

- **Tea and coffee** reduce iron absorption, so are not recommended until your child is much older.
- **Yoghurts** marketed for children can be high in sugar.
- Also be aware that **fruit pots** are very sweet, so try diluting them in plain yoghurt.
- Avoid **'E' numbers** which can make some children over active and out of control.
- **Strawberries** and **kiwis** can rarely cause a skin reaction or eczema. If your baby does get a skin rash a food diary is very helpful.

Allow plenty of time for meals, try to eat with them and at least stop everything to sit down and concentrate on feeding so that your baby has your undivided attention (so much easier with your first child!). Their food initially does look and possibly smell, unappetising but to them it is delicious so smile and tell them enthusiastically how 'yummy' it is. Make meal times fun: chat to them, play games. You do have to sit for a while during meal times which can become boring so it is really up to you to make some fun of this time. Encourage your baby to try and eat a wide varied diet and to stop when they have had enough, not necessarily when the bowl is empty. Meal times can be messy – try to relax about this as it is all part of your baby's learning development. Bibs, floor mats and washing machines will help. When you start weaning, your baby's stool/poo will change. They may become constipated in which case adding fruit or more water works well (see Constipation in the medical index for further advice). They may also increase the number of dirty nappies. This is all normal.

Some children will always be fussy, and you will need to be more inventive with what you feed them and how you present it. Most children, though, are just testing what the rules are, and seeing how they can get more of your attention! Some babies only like finger food and refuse spoons. You may need to be very inventive to get them eating. Sometimes a little bit of food between meals can affect their appetite, so avoid giving them something in between meals when you first start weaning, except for their regular milk, to encourage them to eat at meal time. Unless they are losing weight or showing signs of an illness, try not to worry if they don't eat much. Some babies may need a supplement of iron due to their poor diet but if you are concerned, ask your doctor.

If they really do not like a particular food then give it a miss for a week or two and reintroduce it, possibly in a different way. It may take a few goes for them to like it. If they do not eat their meal, do not cook something else. Give them some fruit and/or yoghurt then try offering the meal after. You can also offer them the original meal later when they are very hungry, or offer something you know they will eat at the next meal. If you are cooking something new then try offering it with foods that your baby does eat.

When you start weaning, avoid biscuits and sweets. If they have never tasted chocolate or sweets they will not know what they are missing! Introduce them when they are older and not every day as this may make your baby less likely to eat savoury and healthy food. If you use biscuits or cakes as rewards for finishing their main course, you may be giving them the message that the main meal is a chore and not so nice. A reward could be anything from a sticker, a star on a chart to a celebratory song, rather than food. And stick to your guns: do not give the reward unless they have done everything you have requested!

If you can prepare all your food at home it is definitely better as you have control over the ingredients. Don't get disheartened if your baby enjoys a certain meal one week and then refuses it the next. It may happen to you!

SLEEPING

(SEE: A ROUGH GUIDE TO THE NUMBER OF FEEDS AND AMOUNT OF SLEEP BABIES NEED EACH DAY)

This is the big one: <u>sleep is so precious for everyone involved</u>. **Newborn babies** need to feed regularly so they **do not sleep though the night. About four hours is the maximum they should have without a feed in the first few weeks**. Your baby does need to be fed at night, so try and make it all as comfortable and pleasurable as possible for yourself. Your newborn baby will not be little for very long so have patience. They all learn to sleep eventually, even if the long nights feel endless to start with.

Like all of us, babies have a sleep-wake cycle. The sleep cycle starts with light sleep then goes into deep sleep for about 20-30 minutes then light again and they wake up. Each cycle lasts about 40-60 minutes. Sometimes your baby may wake up while switching between the two cycles and need quiet settling – not food – to go into the deep sleep. If your baby wakes up after a short sleep and is very grumpy then possibly they missed their deep sleep. Next time try just resettling and reassuring your baby with minimal contact.

As your baby gets older it does not need so much sleep. Check if they may have slept too much during the day and then are just not tired when you want them to sleep at night. Your baby may need to go to bed later if it is waking too early for you.

Your baby's room

Make sure your baby's room is a nice temperature to sleep in – somewhere between **16 degrees to 20 degrees centigrade**. Also a bit of ventilation is good so, if you can, open a window just a little. Some people rave about black-out curtains but the majority of babies sleep well without them. A good sleep routine is far more important. However, if black-out curtains work for your child and get you a few more precious hours' sleep then use them.

When you put your baby into their cot **lay them on their backs** so they look up at the ceiling. Not on their front or side – this is all about avoiding Sudden Infant Death Syndrome or cot deaths (*see* **SIDS**). Make sure their cot is in a safe place: for example, check that there are no strings from curtains that they can touch. Have very little in their cot and ensure there is nothing for them to get caught in.

It is recommended to have your baby in your room for the first 6 months. This is the ideal situation but if it stops you or your partner from sleeping then review your plans as rested parents are happy parents.

Daytime sleep

Babies need lots of little naps during the day as they get tired very easily, so try and space these out between feeds. Some babies have strong preferences about the timing of these sleeps; others will be easier. Your baby can have a daytime sleep anywhere, and if you wrap up your baby snugly (bearing in mind their temperature), it will be a signal to them that it is sleep time. They do not necessarily need to be in a dark room, they will be tired and just need the chance to be quiet.

Settling down to sleep

A good evening routine works well to get your baby off to sleep at night. Try and make everything calm and quiet at this time of the evening, with the minimum of fuss. Give your baby a bath, then a feed so they are ready to go to sleep. Place your baby in the crib or cot calmly and confidently and leave your baby to settle itself. Some babies find music very calming at this time of night. Others love the sound of 'shh' repeated, as this is similar to the noise of your blood vessels working when they were inside you. Some just need peace and quiet. Also regarding lighting – some like a little light some like darkness so try different things.

Crying

If your baby starts crying as soon as you lie them down in the cot, check:

- Their nappy is clean
- They are well-fed (a small extra five-minute feed sometimes helps)
- They do not need winding
- They are not in pain (especially colic and reflux). Reflux can present as persistent crying on being laid down each time – see your doctor.
- Teething
- They are not ill
- *See also* **Crying**

Should you leave your baby to cry? If so - How long can you leave your baby to cry in its cot?

These are very difficult questions to answer and there is really no right answer. It is most important to do what you want to do so if you want to cuddle or carry your baby around with you while your baby falls off to sleep then that is fine. If you do not want to do this; try following this bit of advice to help them to settle in their cot.

If you are feeling very tired and emotional yourself then leaving your baby to cry is the hardest thing and is more than likely to set you off too. Firstly go through the checklist above. Settle your baby down calmly. Then try and leave him or her for a good 5 to 10 minutes. Go back just to check on your baby; try not to lift them out of the cot unless they are inconsolable, in which case pick your baby up and calm them with a reassuring cuddle before putting them back in the cot with minimum fuss. If your baby settles quickly in your arms they just needed a bit of reassuring then they can settle themselves again. Put them back in the cot and leave them again just checking every 10-20 minutes or so. When you do check on your baby, try to see your baby without them seeing you. Find jobs to do at this time such as sort the washing out or start cooking or watch a DVD or your favourite TV show as listening to your baby cry is so depressing. There is also no point getting cross and angry with your baby if he or she is not settling, it will not help and you will just get even more exhausted, some babies are just poor sleepers.

You could also try baby massage, just stroking them or rubbing their soles of the feet through the blankets. You do not need to be trained in anything so long as you are gentle and do what calms your baby down.

If your baby has been ill for a few nights and their sleep has been affected, they may start to cry more at bedtime even when they're better. Persevere with your usual bedtime to help them get back into their usual sleep pattern. The sooner you do this the less likely you will have a sleep problem on your hands.

Bedding
Do not have a duvet, quilt or pillow in your baby's cot. If your baby gets their head down into any of these they are at risk of a cot death. Your baby is also at risk of cot death if it is overheated or too cold.

The easiest option is a sleeping bag which it the right size for your baby. Then put your baby in a sleep suit with a vest or aerated blanket over the top as needed.

If you like sheets and blankets, place your baby with its feet at the feet end of the cot so if your baby wriggles it ends up out of the covers rather than under the covers. Keep the cotton sheet away from their cheeks as if it rubs their cheeks they may start to suckle and wake up.

Avoid having any cot side decorations for two reasons: firstly to avoid your baby getting caught up in them. Secondly because babies use their head to let heat out which helps to regulate their body temperature so if they wriggle and reach the cot side decorations it could prevent your baby losing heat from its head and then overheating.

Tog ratings tell you how well an item will keep you warm. The higher the value of the tog, the warmer it will be.

A 0.5 tog is a lightweight sleeping bag for hot weather and/or a very warm nursery.

A 2.5 tog is suitable for the rest of the year, and your baby may need a warm top for their arms or a blanket made from cotton or wool in cold weather.

Below is a rough guide to tog ratings:

Clothing and bedding

Clothing and bedding	Tog value
Nappy	2
Vest	1
Bodysuit	1
Jumper/cardigan	2
Trousers	2
Sleep suit	4
Single sheet	0.2 (higher if swaddled)
New blanket	2

The recommended total is about 9 togs in a room temperature of 16-20°C. Air temperature also has to be taken into consideration.

- The total tog value is the sum of <u>all</u> the layers of clothes and bedding on your baby.

- Be careful to not over- or under-dress your baby in bed or at any time of the day. Newborns in particular are unable to regulate their own temperature and can overheat easily.

- Swaddling will roughly **treble** the tog value, so some judgement is needed here. Feeling the back of your baby's neck with the back of your hand can give you a clue about how warm your baby is.

- In heat of over 24°C, your baby will only need a light cover. Some babies are so hot they just need to sleep in their nappy. At cooler temperatures (18-24°C) they will need about one bodysuit and a light blanket or sheet swaddle, some babies may need another light blanket. Below 18°C your baby will need two or more blankets. Cold little hands can be normal.

- During the day remember to remove warm hats and extra clothes when you go indoors or into a car, train or shop. This is very important if the room is warm – even if it means waking up your baby. Babies lose their excess heat from their heads. Also make sure they're wearing a hat outside on cooler days.

CRYING

All babies cry – it is how they communicate and get your attention. It is how they express being cold/hungry/wet, but it's also the only noise they can make, to start with, and it's good for them to exercise their lungs!

It's easy to feel anxious when your baby is yelling their head off, especially when you're out and about, but try and remember that although it sounds earth-shattering to you; your baby's cry really isn't that loud to anyone else. A little cry does them no harm at all and as long as they are safe, you can leave your baby to cry a little. Sometimes you just have to do things such as get your shopping in from the car. Put your baby down in a safe place, get yourself sorted then pick your baby up again. You will feel so much more in control and relaxed rather than trying to do both at the same time.

It is easy to be more attentive with your first child, but if you go on to have more, often you have no choice but to let them cry and go to them when you can. If you pick your baby up the second they make a noise, your baby might become unnecessarily fussy. Trust your instincts as a mother – you will learn to recognise when they are distressed rather than just a bit grouchy.

There are many reasons why a baby might be crying, and often it's a combination of things, or none – it is often a case of trial and error. To start with, though, check the following:

- **Dirty nappy**. Always check, even if you can't smell anything.
- **Hungry**. If they are hungry think about how much you have fed them so far in the day and when they were last fed – see if your little finger to suck on can keep them happy.
- **Thirsty**. If it is hot, try some cooled boiled water. It is important to think of this if they are being bottle-fed, as bottle-fed babies are more likely to be dehydrated or constipated and water will help. Breastfed babies generally do not need extra water.
- **Winded**. Is there another bubble present? (*See* **Winding**).
- **Temperature**. The room should be 16-20°C – babies complain of being too cold more often than too hot; when they're too hot they just become drowsy. Be careful not to overheat babies with too many clothes (especially in hot shops) or having the heating up too high. Feeling the skin on the back of their neck or tummy will give you a clue of their body temperature. (*See* **Tog Ratings**.)
- **Teething. (***See*** Teething.)**
- **Pain.** This is the most important to exclude – they generally have their knees up to their chest and look distressed. Often it is caused by colic (*see* **Colic**). There are many causes of pains so ask your doctor if you are concerned.
- **Over-tired or over-stimulated**. Your baby needs to sleep in the day even if he or she is sleeping well at night. On the other hand, he/she may just need to be left alone in their cot to settle themselves. Sometimes all the rocking and singing is just keeping them awake.
- **Bored during wake times.** Mobiles and play-mats with things that dangle down, mirrors and shiny bits

that catch the light are great when very small. More interactive things are needed when they are a bit bigger. What they really want, though, is your attention and for you to play with them. They also love their toes so let them have a play without their socks sometimes during the day.

- **Reassurance.** The world is so new to your baby sometimes they just need a cuddle.

If you are at all concerned, for example if the crying is inconsolable, unusual or you just are worrying then don't hesitate to consult a doctor.

If your baby is crying and you get to a point where you cannot cope with it then phone a friend or your health visitor. **Never shake your baby** as this causes them harm. If you feel that you are at this level of desperation then put your baby down in a cot where he or she is safe and wait for whoever you have called to come. Do not be ashamed to ask for help – everyone who's had a baby knows how hard it can be.

Cry-sis.org.uk or phone 08451 228669 is a support for families with excessively crying, sleepless and demanding babies run by parents who have gone through similar experiences.

Ideas to help stop crying

Sometimes just holding your baby in a different position or a gentle back rub helps. Some love music; others love being rocked. On going to sleep saying 'shh... shh... shh' continuously in their ear may calm them, as might gentle rolling from side to side while in their cot.

Taking them for a walk may help – often the change in temperature and fresh air calms them down (as well as you). A trip in the car can lull your baby off to sleep, too. I don't recommend using either of these tips to get them to sleep at night though, as they can start a habit of evening excursions that you might have to continue for months. As all parents discover, necessity can make you end up doing all sorts of things! If you have a baby who cries a lot and is very tense and unsettled, try baby massage or craniosacral osteopathy; some parents have found it very helpful for their baby.

HYGIENE and BATHING

Nappies

Nappy-changing is pretty straightforward when your baby is very small (once you get the hang of it), but as they become more mobile and wriggly it can become quite a task to perform! The more you do the easier it gets. A changing mat is essential. If you have a wriggly baby, the floor is the safest place to change them. If you do put your baby on a surface, never let go of your baby. Check the changing surface is a good height for your back and make sure you are not twisting at odd angles.

Always wipe from front (tummy) to back (bottom). Place as much stool in the toilet as you can. Wipe with cotton wool dipped in warm water – this is ideal but not always practical so baby wipes are great. Then the most important step is to dry the nappy area – either with a clean towel or a tissue/toilet roll. Check the skin is touch dry, including all the creases and under the folds and the buttocks. Then place on the next nappy. The gathers go at the back, look at the pictures on the nappy if unsure. Secure the nappy with the side stickers to the front; they need to be firm but not too tight. Avoid baby powder as it can irritate their lungs. Always remember to wash your hands afterwards to avoid infections.

If you can afford the environmentally friendly biodegradable nappies then buy those, otherwise use standard disposable nappies. If you are up for the non-disposables, they are great and they do save you money. They do however need changing more regularly and there is more washing to do. In some areas there is a nappy service which your health visitor may be able to advise you. Sometimes a disposable nappy at night can help because the non-disposables can get cold and wet and wake your baby up.

Boys and girls

A **boy's** scrotal sac may be very large when he is first born. Be careful to clean under it. Their little penis can fly around when passing urine so watch out –make sure it is pointing down when you finish changing a nappy or you might both end up wet! The foreskin is not expected to retract until they are about three to five years old so don't start cleaning under it until then.

Girls' vaginal area: Do check, and clean out any poo that gets in, but do not over-clean. Just water on some cotton wool is ideal. Wipes are fine but can irritate the skin. When first born some white debris may be present – clean this away gently in the bath over a few days. Always clean from front (tummy) to back (bottom) one way; if you need to clean more then use another cotton wool ball or a fresh wipe. Girls are prone to urinary tract infections and this is one thing that can help prevent them.

Nappy Rash

Causes:

- Nappies left on too long
- Sensitive skin
- Certain soaps, detergent or bubble bath
- Baby wipes containing alcohol and perfume
- Diarrhoea or general illnesses
- Teething
- Changing diet either from breast milk to formula or when weaning.

How to Look after Nappy Rash:

- Make sure the skin is touch dry at all times; frequent nappy changes help.
- Lay your baby on a mat without a nappy on, to let the air on it – you could put a small towel on the changing mat. Watch out: they can pass urine and poo more often than you realise!
- Use barrier cream – get advice from your pharmacist.
- Barrier creams are only needed if a rash is present, should be used thinly and are not necessarily needed every day.
- If your baby has a recurrent nappy rash, try an emollient (cream) regularly after every nappy change.
- If none of this works then see your GP for advice as there may be a Candida/thrush infection.

Stools/poo: what colour?

Meconium is the first substance passed from your baby's bottom. It is **green-black** and sticky/greasy. It is usually passed in the first 12 hours, although it can be delayed in some normal babies, and has generally gone by day three. If your baby has not passed meconium in the first 24 hours or has not passed urine then your baby needs urgent medical advice.

The nappies then turn **green and watery** until the milk comes in about day three to five.

If you are breastfeeding, your baby's stool will be **yellow/orange and runny**, odourless and usually three to four times a day. It can be as often as after every feed but the other extreme is once a week. I advise that up to five days without opening bowels can be normal and put down to constipation provided your baby is well. However, you should seek medical advice if you are at all concerned.

If you are using formula/bottle-feeding, the stool will be **pale brown**, may be very smelly and can be **hard**, causing your baby to strain. If the straining is causing rectal (bottom) bleeding or the bowels are opening only every two or more days, this is constipation (*see **Constipation***).

Black stool can be caused by iron supplements. If your baby is not taking an iron supplement then see your doctor to discuss.

Frequent stool can be normal if your baby is gaining weight and the stools look normal, though if this persists after six months then consult your doctor for a check-up.

Umbilical Cord

When your baby is first born the cord is soft. After a few days it will become hard and then eventually drop off, generally by day ten. To help this, always place the umbilical cord outside the nappy, even if you have to turn down the top of the nappy to do it. Make sure it is dried after bath time – tissues will help. A few drops of lavender oil in a little water dabbed on with cotton wool or a tissue can also help the umbilical cord dry, especially if it becomes soggy-looking. When the umbilical cord falls off most will leave an inward tummy button but some stick out. Most of these 'outies' will sort themselves out by the time your baby is one year old.

Umbilical Granuloma

This is an overgrowth of tissue in the belly button which can occur after the umbilical cord drops off. It is soft, pink and shiny. To treat it keep it clean and dry and roll down the nappy to let the air at it. Then put some table/cooking salt over the granuloma with a gauze dressing on top and leave for 30 minutes then wash off. Repeat this twice a day for about 3 days. It is does not settle or has an offensive smell or discharge then see your doctor.

Teeth and Teething

Normal teeth development can range from your baby being born with teeth to not having any until after their first birthday. In general:

First Teeth (Deciduous)		Appearance (months)
Central incisor (Front teeth)	Lower	6-10
	Upper	7-10
Lateral Incisor	Upper	8-10
	Lower	12-18
First Molar		12-18
Canine		16-20
Second Molar		20-30

Preventative dental care is important from the day they are born. Firstly **babies need milk or water ONLY until they**

are four to six months old. **AVOID** giving your baby **sugary drinks or fruit juice.**

After six months, if you want to give them a fruit juice then dilute it and give it to them in a beaker, not a bottle. If they taste the sweet drinks then they will want them: what they don't know about they will not want.

Find other treats such as a sticker, a crayon, a small book or reading them a story rather than sweets. They are easily pleased when very young.

Try to clean their teeth last thing at night after the last milk feed. Start cleaning with a toothbrush and a very tiny bit of (age-appropriate) toothpaste as soon as your baby's first teeth arrive, so that they get used to having their teeth cleaned.

Teething

Teething can start at any age but generally at about six months. It can present with lots of different symptoms such as dribbling, biting, red cheek(s), change in stool, nappy rash, bit grizzly, bad breath or being off their food. It can be painful for them so try:

- a teething ring
- rubbing their gums with your finger
- hard vegetables to chew on such as raw carrot or a soothing cucumber
- cold food sometimes can be more soothing than warm foods
- use gels to rub on the gums from your pharmacist
- paracetamol
- Homeopathic remedies which you can buy at pharmacies or from a homeopath

---

If your baby accidentally knocks its tooth out then put it in a glass of milk and go straight to your dentist. If a tooth is chipped then you just have to wait for the next set of teeth when they are about six years old.

Bath time

The only rule to bathing children is to **watch them all the time**. Do not look away, have everything ready before you put them in the bath and take them out of the bath if you need to leave the room. Take no chances. Ignore the phone or doorbell; alternatively take your baby with you.

When your baby is first born it is important **not** to wash it straight away as there is a risk they will get too cold. It should be safe to wash your baby after an hour or so after the birth so long as the room is warm and the towels are warm. Your baby will be covered in a creamy, greasy covering called vernix – this washes off very easily or if left will be absorbed naturally. Their hair, if they have any, also only needs water to get it clean. Your baby may have fine hair on its body; this will mostly go by the time they are about one to two months old. Try to avoid other products until your baby is older; anything that touches the skin is absorbed into the body. Look out for all the folds – particularly under their chins, behind their ears and in their hands; they all need cleaning and drying.

They may have dry flaky skin – do not peel it off, wait for it to fall off naturally. Their nails can be long: trim them using your teeth or fine nail clippers but go carefully. You could try cutting their nails when they are asleep but look after your back if you bend over a cot to do this.

A small baby bath – which they will use for around two to three months – can make bathing your baby easier. Alternatively you can put about 3-5cm of water in a normal-sized bath; they can lie in this unaided but you **must** be watching all the time. A baby flannel support or bath seat is excellent and can be used up to about six months. If you use these you still need to keep watching your baby in the bath.

Buy a bath thermometer as it is very difficult to guess the right temperature for your baby (36-38°C); check with your elbow if you are confident. Wash them with water only. To hold them in the bath, put your left (if right-handed) arm under your baby's head and hold their upper arm/armpit furthest away from you, with your fingers and thumb. Look after your back while doing this.

If your baby does not like having baths then don't do it! Keep your life easy and just use a wet flannel with your baby lying on a towel.

Washing clothes

To wash your baby's clothes, use a non-biological washing powder and a germicidal non-biological pre-wash or soak such as Napisan.

It is also ok to use biological washing powder, but change to non-biological if your baby has dry, itchy or red skin. Sometimes your baby will be able to tolerate one kind of washing powder but have a reaction to another. You will need a pre-wash or soak for any vomit or poo; it will wash off better if soaked first and not allowed to dry. Soak for, ideally, 6 to 24 hours then put through a wash. If your baby has very sensitive skin then try re-rinsing the washes. If possible hang out yellow poo-stained clothes, after washing them, in direct sunlight and this will help get rid of the staining.

3: YOU - Your Body, Your Emotions

NOTES FOR MOTHERS

Congratulations on becoming a mother! In this section, my aim in this section is to help you recover from childbirth and to enjoy those first few months with your baby. Your baby will not do much for the first few weeks or months. Some of you will just love every minute and others will feel it is relentless or boring, but that's all ok.

Complications after birth

It is rare to get serious complications from childbirth but if you experience any of the following symptoms after giving birth, you must seek medical treatment **straight away**:

● Sudden or heavy vaginal blood loss

- Severe headache, or headache on sitting up or standing
- Blurred vision
- High blood pressure
- Shortness of breath or chest pain
- Calf pain
- Very high temperature – over 38°C
- Suicidal thoughts
- Agitation, confusion and delusions – see <u>puerperal psychosis</u>

If you have any of the following then please seek medical treatment; these can generally **wait until the next day**:

- Smelly vaginal discharge
- Very tender or painful lower abdomen/tummy
- Piles that are painful
- Perineal pain (pain between your vaginal and anus) and/or smelly painful urine
- Leaking from your bottom or having no control of your bowel/stool movements
- Baby blues that have gone on longer than ten days.

REST

Just after you have given birth you need to rest and look after yourself, and that means letting others around you help. Your partner can have a very useful role by helping to shop, cook and clean. They can also help by bathing your baby, changing their nappy and taking them for a walk while you sleep or rest.

If you feel overwhelmed it is because you are exhausted.

You are not used to getting up throughout the night and this takes up a huge amount of energy from you, as does breastfeeding.

New mothers are always amazed how exhausting it is looking after such a tiny thing. If you achieve one thing a day, you have done well! Getting dressed could be this one thing! Eating well is very important.

PELVIC RECOVERY

Labour is so painful, but once your baby is born most of the pain suddenly goes (*also see* **After a Caesarian Section**). You may have needed a few sutures (stitches). This is to help hold together any small or large tears in your vaginal area while it heals. This can be painful so you may want the gas and air and a few good breaths but midwives/hospital doctors are very quick. Stitches generally dissolve within three to four weeks after birth although some sutures are designed to last longer.

After this you are encouraged to get up and have a bath/shower which is generally very welcome. Beware – your vaginal area will be very sore and swollen. You will be bleeding so go prepared for your bath or shower with towels/toilet paper to dry up the blood while you get on your disposable pants with a large sanitary towel in it. This is all very messy but it has to be done and you do feel better after. You will need to change your sanitary pad very often initially then less often as the days go on. Always remove your pad from front to back to avoid passing any infections from your anal area.

The bleeding in the first three to four days will be the worst. If the bleeding is not showing signs of settling or you are passing clots or flooding the pads very quickly then please seek medical advice. By two weeks the bleeding should be very little, and it should stop completely by about four to six weeks. Change your maternity pads regularly to help your vaginal area heal faster. There should be no foul smell. If you have a foul, offensive smell in your vaginal area it may indicate an infection which will need treatment. Do not use tampons as these can cause infection. If you have no vaginal bleeding in the first 2 weeks this may need urgent medical care.

Passing urine after birth can be difficult but you should pass urine within 6-8 hours after birth. It may sting after giving birth. Drinking lots of water will help as it dilutes the urine; even though you may go more often it will not hurt as much. Standing up over the toilet may help you to pass urine without it touching your sore areas. Passing urine in a bath can be soothing. Pouring warm water over your vaginal area after you have been to the toilet can be very soothing and better than just using toilet paper. This is where your small plastic jug gets used. You should have control on passing urine straight away although your urine may not flow out in a straight line after delivery; this generally sorts itself out with time. A little bit of incontinence – where urine leaks out when you are not expecting it – is normal, but if you are flooding yourself with urine without control then that is important to discuss this with your midwife or doctor.

Your bowels could take a few days to work again, (*see* **Managing and Avoiding Constipation**) and **keep mobile** or discuss this with your doctor or midwife. Ask for advice early.

The sooner you can start doing pelvic floor exercises, the better (*see* **Your Pelvic Floor**).

PELVIC CARE
When you start moving around after you've given birth, your pelvic and vaginal areas will feel sore and swollen. The good news is that it will get better over the next few days (worst case is about four weeks). Vaginal pain after delivery can be very severe for some of you. It will go but here are some things that might help:

- Keep changing your sanitary pads regularly and keep the area as dry as possible.

- Wear loose cotton clothing to help healing.
- Drink plenty of water to keep your urine diluted.
- Sitting on condoms that have been filled with water and frozen! This sounds strange, but some find they are the perfect shape to sit on and soothe the swelling.
- Lavender oil or tea tree oil – a few drops in your bath or a few drops on your sanitary pad can be very soothing. It does not sting but do not apply directly.
- Arnica cream applied to the sanitary pad can be very soothing.
- Some mums have found homeopathy helpful.

If your vaginal area is not improving then please seek medical advice.

If you have the odd area that is very tender then seek medical advice. Sometimes the sutures can be too tight or you may have a small infection.

VAGINAL TEARS
There are three types of vaginal tear:

First degree
This describes small superficial tears in the skin of the perineum (about 1.5cm maximum). Many of these just heal. They may sting for a few days. If they are more painful than that then you may have an infection so ask either your midwife or doctor to check your perineum.

Second degree
This is a larger tear that involves the vaginal wall and muscles and skin. An episiotomy cuts through the vaginal wall and muscles but it is used to direct the stress of the perineum in childbirth away from the anus. These tears or cuts need suturing. Sometimes the sutures can be too tight or the scarring tissue narrows the vagina. Both can be painful and can make intercourse difficult. This can be

surgically corrected but gentle stretching and massage is usually all that is needed.

Third degree
This is where the anal sphincter or muscles are torn or cut during childbirth. It is repaired with sutures straight away and most heal well. While healing it is important to take a laxative regularly and not to become constipated or to strain when opening your bowels. Faecal incontinence (passing stool/poo without control) and flatulence (wind) are common problems following a third-degree tear. These problems may not occur straight away after giving birth. If it is a significant problem you may benefit from surgery later on. Pelvic floor exercises including the anal muscles will also help. Other problems that occur include a **scarred perineum**. Regular massage with almond or olive oil over several months may help soften this. Extra lubrication may be needed for intercourse.

AFTER PAINS
No one ever warns you about these! They are pains from your uterus while it contracts. It can be especially sharp after delivery and go on for about two weeks before they ease off. The pain can catch you especially when you breastfeed. To cope with them, remember the breathing exercises from your antenatal classes. Breathing in and out slowly does help.

AFTER A CAESAREAN SECTION
A Caesarean Section is a major operation so it will take time to heal. Afterwards you may be in a surprising amount of pain and feel you cannot do anything. Holding your wound with your hand or a pillow can help you to move. Wear clothes and underwear that are loose and comfortable. Keep your wound clean and dry. If it becomes painful and red or oozes then ask your midwife or doctor to look at it as it may have an infection and need treatment. The scar line may get a lump underneath

which can appear suddenly. Often this is a large collection of blood like a large bruise which then takes days or weeks to disappear.

You will still bleed vaginally, the same as after a vaginal birth. If you had an emergency Section and had a Ventouse or forceps as well you may also have had stitches as above (*see* **Pelvic Recovery** and **Pelvic Care**).

Make sure you do not get constipated.

Ask for painkillers – you may need to take them regularly. Be careful if you are taking a lot of painkillers as you may be unaware of damaging your back or having mastitis or you may get constipated as a side effect.

After a Caesarean Section you should be up and walking within 24 hours. It gets easier the more you move around. You may be very light-headed initially. Keep moving your ankles and legs; otherwise you are at risk of a DVT, which is a blood clot in your lower leg which causes pain, redness and swelling in your calf.

You can breastfeed straight away but you may need help if you are in a lot of pain.

You should not lift anything (including your toddler if you have one), do housework or exercise (except for pelvic floors) for at least the first 6 weeks – which is easier said than done.

You can drive when you feel confident to do an emergency stop. Start doing gentle tummy exercises after 6 weeks. Other more vigorous exercise should not start before 12 weeks. Sometimes you will be left with an over-hang of tummy over the scar. The scar itself generally fades in time.

Some of you will have had a planned Caesarean Section, others will have had an emergency one. You may feel relieved that it is all over and delighted that you can get on and enjoy your new baby. Others, however, might feel upset or disappointed that you didn't give birth vaginally.

You may have had an emotional rollercoaster going through the delivery of your baby and felt totally out of control at such an important moment in your life. Talking this through with the doctors or midwives or counsellors afterwards can really help. The experience can be very traumatic so be kind to yourself and your partner. Caesarean Sections have increased the number of live healthy babies and mothers and they are not done without careful assessment first. Your baby's wellbeing and your health will have been the most important consideration when deciding on the right delivery for you.

YOUR PELVIC FLOOR

The main thing to stress is that **it will all heal!** Some of you, after giving birth, will have significant urinary incontinence (pass urine without control), especially when you jump or cough or sneeze, though most will improve dramatically after a few weeks. For a few of you it will be more serious than that. It's vital to do pelvic floor exercises for months – if not years – to get total control again and prevent urinary incontinence and vaginal prolapse when older.

The goal is to be able to jump up and down without leaking: try a trampoline or skipping. At first you may be hopeless but with regular pelvic floor exercises you can improve significantly. Never stop doing these exercises!

The two sets of pelvic floor exercises:
- **20 short squeezes** Inside your vagina are a bundle of muscles: try to move them up towards your

umbilical/tummy button. You should be able to feel them going up and down. Squeeze then release. Do 20 in quick succession.
- **5 long squeezes** As above, but count to ten (about ten seconds) and release. Do five at a time.

Try and do this at least five times a day. If you are not achieving it then put up notices everywhere – near the kettle, in the bathroom, by the TV, near the changing mat – to remind yourself. It might look strange, but it's better than wetting yourself! Or you could do them every time you change a nappy or feed your baby.

If you are having trouble, you do not know where your pelvic muscles are, or there is no improvement then you need to first feel where your pelvic muscles are with your fingers. So firstly place your fingers inside your vagina and shut your eyes so you can visualise the muscles you are using. This is not easy but keep trying. Then try and squeeze around your fingers. Soon you will know where your pelvic muscles are. Keep doing your exercises regularly, and do them with your **eyes shut**. This will help you regain the connections needed between your brain and your pelvis so your muscles start working automatically. Specialised physiotherapists can be very helpful.

You can do your pelvic floor exercises anywhere but when you start off, if you lie on the floor on your back with your knees bent it can help you find the right muscles.

Your anal muscles can also be used when you are doing your pelvic floor exercises. These can be used separately or in combination with your vaginal muscles. Try to squeeze them all up towards your tummy button. Your lower abdominal muscles can also be involved too. These are the band of muscles between your hips which you can pull in to make yourself look slimmer. So pull in your tummy button and feel those muscles link to your vaginal muscles, bottom muscles and lower abdomen/tummy muscles – then you have really got it.

YOUR TUMMY

Straight after you have given birth your tummy will still look at least six months pregnant if not more. It can be unnerving the first time you stand up having given birth. So take your maternity clothes to wear home from hospital. To get your figure back you may need to put some effort in or you will always be larger than pre-pregnancy. The 'gap' in the stomach muscles down the centre line needs to unite before doing full sit-ups or you may be at increased risk of a hernia forming. Blowing your nose can be very difficult when your tummy muscles are weak! It will be much improved with pelvic floor exercises above and the tummy exercises described next.

Exercises for your tummy

Lie on the floor on your back, maybe even next to your baby and gently get your tummy muscles to move up and down. DO NOT lift your head off the floor to start with. You have three sets of tummy muscles – upper, middle and lower and then the right side and the left side (what's known as a 'six pack'!).

Put your hands on the lower muscles (this is the band that goes across from one hip bone to the other and is below your tummy button), shut your eyes to help try and visualise the muscles working, and squeeze, moving them up and down. Then repeat this for the band of muscles across your tummy button – the middle band. Finally, the upper band which is above your tummy button between your ribs. At first you may not find them but keep going and you will find them all. When you have found them then squeeze each set of muscles 20 times.

When you can move these three sets of muscles, start doing very gentle sit-ups: lie on your back on the floor with your knees bent and lift your head about 10cms only from the floor. Try and repeat this up to 100 times. Initially you will not get past ten, but as the weeks go on you will build up. Try and do this at least once a day.

If you have had a Caesarean Section you can do these exercises but do **not** do the gentle sit-ups until at least six weeks after your baby is born. After a Caesarean Section you need to wait 12 weeks after your baby is born before you start more intense exercises and full sit-ups because your abdominal muscles need time to reunite.

STRETCH
This may sound like an odd thing to do. However, once your baby arrives you'll be spending a lot of time feeding, cuddling, changing nappies and leaning over –all with your shoulders curled inwards. You need to stretch out to breathe properly and unroll your shoulders to help prevent shoulder and back pain. So stand on your tiptoes and reach upwards as high as you can and take a big breath in. Then bring your arms down sideways and breathe out, landing on your feet again. Do about five of these, especially in the morning. It is also a great thing to do when you are feeling overwhelmed. If your baby is crying non-stop and you don't know what to do next, put your baby down in a safe place and take a break with five stretches. Sometimes it can just give you the break you need.

LOSING THE WEIGHT

There are two key parts to losing weight:
exercise and food.

Exercising has to start gently after having a baby. Follow the advice above initially and then build up as the months go on. Take care not to over-exercise as that can affect the quantity of your breast milk if you are breastfeeding.

Breastfeeding helps you lose weight as long as your diet is good. When you are pregnant your body will have gained some extra fat and it will use this to fuel breastfeeding. But if you have a cake every time you breastfeed don't be surprised if you are suddenly gaining weight rather than losing it.

Dieting is not recommended while breastfeeding so try to relax about your figure and wait until you have stopped breastfeeding.

Eating healthy foods is often easier said than done. The less processed your food, the better it will be for you. Healthy foods include fruit, vegetables and nuts (brazils, walnuts, pecans, almonds) and seeds (such as sesame seeds, pumpkin seeds and sunflower seeds), which are all great for snacks. Your body also needs the basics of meat, fish, pulses, grains, potatoes, rice, oats/porridge, dairy and eggs. If you are a vegetarian or vegan, get good advice. Pulses are a must and should be the mainstay of your diet.

When you are at home more, it is easy to get into the habit of having lots of snacks. And when you're very tired you often comfort yourself with food. Healthy snacks will help you and your tiredness more than if you eat the sweet foods.

Ideas of foods to eat

- **Breakfast** – cereals; eggs and toast; yoghurt and fruit and nuts.

- **Main meal and lighter meals** – a variety of meat, pulses or fish with vegetables and potatoes, rice or pasta as you like. Jacket potatoes with your favourite filling. Pitta bread, naan bread or a sandwich with a healthy filling such as humous, cheese, ham or tuna.

Or a salad of your choice. Followed by fruit, yoghurt or pudding but try to avoid processed puddings.

- **Snacks** – try and have healthy ones around such as breadsticks, chapattis, vegetables and humous, fresh or dried fruit, malt loaf, fruit bread or cheese and oatcakes.

Foods to eat in moderation

- **Chocolate** – chocolate might seem a great pick-me-up, but it isn't really. You get a sugar high from it which sadly doesn't last long, followed by a sugar low which makes you more tired and irritable. This goes on until you eat more chocolate – but the more sugar you eat the more tired you also become. High-coco chocolate (70-80 per cent solids) is better for you for two main reasons: the chocolate bar has less sugar; and most people can only eat a little bit of it. A little of what you like is good for you!

- **Caffeine** – no more than three cups a day of either coffee or tea is the general recommendation if you are breastfeeding. You need to drink plenty of water when breastfeeding. Fizzy drinks also contain a lot of caffeine and sugar and there is nothing healthy in them.

- Avoid **high-sugar foods** and foods with **trans-fatty acids** or **hydrogenated fats** in them.

INTERCOURSE AFTER BIRTH

NB: Remember to use birth control/contraception. From three weeks onwards after giving birth, you can become pregnant.

There is no 'normal' time after childbirth to have intercourse – a lot depends on you and your delivery as to when you are ready. It is recommended to wait until you have stopped bleeding, and also that you have no vaginal discharge and no fever. If you had an episiotomy then you need to wait three to five weeks for it to heal fully; if you had a Caesarean Section you need to wait for the incision to heal (about four to six weeks). Some advise no intercourse until six weeks after birth but there is no evidence behind this time except that by six weeks your uterus should have returned to its normal size.

Intercourse can be painful initially, especially if you had stitches or perineal damage. It may take you several months to recover from childbirth and it is normal for some couples not to have sexual intercourse for six months to a year. Careful gentle positioning at intercourse can help. Vaginal dryness is very common especially in the first three months or if you are breastfeeding due to lower oestrogen levels and good lubricating jelly from the pharmacist can help. The lower levels of oestrogen may also lower your libido, something that is also affected by postnatal depression and self-consciousness of your postnatal body. Another common cause of painful intercourse after birth is a condition called vaginismus where the vaginal muscles spasm, making penetration in particular very painful. This is treatable with the help of a physiotherapist who specialises in women's health.

Painful intercourse can also be caused by the scarring or an odd suture which can be reversed with massage or a simple operation. Ask your doctor for an assessment and advice however embarrassed you are as it is an important problem.

It is important to talk to your partner about how you feel and what hurts even if you find it an embarrassing conversation to have. It may help him understand why you are not interested in intercourse and reassure him. If you do have intercourse you may find that you have less sexual sensation and less satisfaction. Doing your pelvic floors will help you tone up your vaginal muscles and also help increase your sensitivity. Relax, do not rush and be patient.

CONTRACEPTION
Contraception is not needed for the first 21 days after childbirth – but after that you need to use something or your next baby may arrive ten months after this one! Options include the progesterone-only pill, which is safe to use when breastfeeding. If you are bottle-feeding then the combined oral contraceptive pill is a good option. The intra-uterine device (IUD) or coil, implant or depo injection are other very good options and can all be discussed with your doctor. Condoms are equally effective when used correctly – the penis drips semen when erect so the penis must always have a condom on when it is near your vaginal area. The condom must be removed from the erect penis or the semen can escape down the sides. The 'withdrawal' method fails regularly and is only fine if you don't mind getting pregnant again. Sterilisation is irreversible. Some say that vasectomies can be reversed – some can but most cannot. Tubal sterilisations are also very hard to reverse so think carefully before proceeding with this option.

BREAST PROBLEMS

Nipple pain
Nipple/breast pain is the pain that you may get during those first few gulps of breast milk – for some this can be eye-wateringly painful, although many will have no problems at all. This initial pain you get every time you breastfeed in the

early days can make you tense up before latching on. Try and keep going: it **does** settle in time. The pain should only last the first few gulps then you can enjoy the rest of the feed. Slow breathing does help – try taking a sharp, deep breath in as your baby latches on.

It really is worth trying to continue breastfeeding if you can. But if the pain continues while breastfeeding then **STOP** and start again. It is better to take your baby off five times and try and find the right position than to risk cracked nipples.

Cracked nipples
Cracked nipples are a common complaint of breastfeeding. Poor positioning when feeding or feeding for too long are the most common causes. After each feed try covering the nipple with a little of the breast milk and let it dry. Avoid soaps as this dries the skin. Change your breast pads regularly. Try sleeping topless on a thick towel as this lets the air get to your nipples. There are some excellent creams which may help; ask your pharmacist or midwife. If it is extremely painful you can always feed on the same breast for two feeds in a row to give the cracked one a chance to recover.

Nipple thrush
Nipple thrush is a very painful condition. It can present in many ways: for example, severe shooting or stabbing pains in both or one breast for up to two hours after each feed. This pain can radiate round to your armpits or your back. The pain is generally less during the feed. Your nipples can become very sensitive especially to temperature changes such as cold or hot water. Your nipples may be itchy or have some tiny blisters or look shiny. Occasionally your nipples can be cracked but refusing to heal. Treatment is by oral antifungal for 10 to 14 days and treating your baby with an oral gel too to stop re-infection.

Freezing fresh milk does not kill the spores so it can re-infect your baby who then in turn passes it back to you. All frozen milk or expressed milk needs to be thrown away. Increase your hygiene so all your clothes and hands are washed regularly.

Engorgement

Breast engorgement occurs once the milk comes in, from day three to five, and mainly occurs just before or soon after starting feeding. So long as the whole breast is engorged – not just one area – then it is normal. Your breasts are full of milk. It can be painful: massaging the breasts and either heat or the cold (such as hot baths, hot flannels, hot water bottles, hot grain bags or 'soft' frozen ice packs) may help to relieve the pain. Also expressing a little milk can help ease the engorgement and soften your nipple, this also may help your baby to suckle.

Savoy cabbage leaves in your bra can help engorgement even if it does look odd! There is no scientific proof or an explanation but if you do want to try cabbage leaves then wash, dry and cool the leaves first. Put the leaves in a fan around your breast avoiding contact with your nipple. Cabbage leaves can reduce your milk supply.

Mastitis and how to avoid it

Mastitis is an infection in the milk ducts of the breast. The area of breast affected will be red, hot and very painful. You will also possibly have a fever and be aching too. You may need antibiotics: most of the antibiotics suitable can be taken when breastfeeding, so do not stop. Very occasionally you may develop an abscess – this may need surgical treatment.

Some mothers are just unlucky and are prone to mastitis. You may get it very early on and end up giving up

---

breastfeeding. If you are one of these mothers there is not a lot you can do to change this so don't feel guilty.

Things to do

- Firstly be aware of mastitis. When your breasts become engorged, it should feel 'even' throughout the breast – not just full in one area. If you get an area of breast that feels more engorged/sensitive/full than the rest of the breast, this is an at-risk area. The main thing is to massage the area. Ideally you need to feel your breasts at the end of every feed and when you have a bath or shower to check there is no 'full' area.
- Massage the area of breast that is lump or tender – always massaging towards the nipple.
- Use breastfeeding to release this area. The biggest suck is from the lower jaw of your baby so move your baby so its lower jaw/chin is in the line of the blockage to the nipple. This can lead to interesting feeding angles but your baby feeding this way is very effective.
- Have a really hot bath and soak in it, then start massaging your breasts – especially the tender/at risk areas – always towards the nipple. Soon you will get breast milk squirting out of the nipple. Keep going until that area is soft – this can take a good five to ten minutes. When massaging you may have to press quite hard to help release this pressure. One way is to use the tips of your fingers in a rotational manner over the area, the other is to put your hand in a fist and roll your knuckles over the area – always towards the nipple. Do each at-risk area in turn. Do not worry about lost milk – it all helps you make more. If the breast is really painful you could need about three baths a day in the acute phase.
- Use the electric breast pump and massage the at-risk area at the same time (you may find you don't have enough hands for this!)

- There are specialised physiotherapists who can also help with treating mastitis.
- Some mums have found homeopathy helpful.

COMMON MEDICAL PROBLEMS AFTER BIRTH

Back pain
Back pain is very common after birth, and many of you will have had sore backs throughout pregnancy. Physiotherapy can be very effective; otherwise a recommended osteopath or chiropractor can help. Try to exercise and keep moving. Also make sure you have a good back support when you feed and look after your posture – keep stretching. Good abdomen and pelvic muscles (core muscles) also helps strengthen and support your back. Some people find Pilates or yoga good for strengthening these; gentle swimming can also help. Be very careful how you pick up your baby especially from a cot or when using the car seat; think of your posture first, and remember to bend your knees.

Haemorrhoids
These are common especially towards the end of pregnancy and just after delivery. They can be very uncomfortable. There is also no great treatment for them except waiting for them to go away. If you have them then keep your anal area very clean and dry. You can use creams, ointments and suppositories to help take the pain away. Applying heat or cold to the area can be soothing. Try and make sure you do not get constipated, strain or pass hard stools.

Straight after childbirth, sitting on an ice pack can be very soothing for piles. There is a 'rubber ring' designed to take the pressure off the anal area but it is not recommended for more than a couple of days as actually sitting and putting pressure on that area will help reduce the swellings. It will get better and most disappear within a few weeks.

Managing and Avoiding Constipation:
- Drink extra water
- Eat more fruit and vegetables - prunes, oranges, apples, kiwi. Bananas can both help constipation or cause constipation
- Extra protein such as red meat can help some of you
- Chocolate or caffeine for some can stimulate the bowel
- One teaspoon to one tablespoon three times a day of linseed oil daily can be very effective
- See your doctor regarding medicines for constipation

Everyone is different so you need to find out what works for you.

Anaemia
This is very common and often overlooked. It can easily be remedied by taking iron tablets. Consider the possibility of anaemia if you are slate-grey in colour (look at photos of yourself) or if you are excessively tired or always short of breath walking up stairs. Your doctor can do a simple blood test to check.

Postnatal fever
This indicates you either have an infection in your vagina, urine or breast, or you have a non-infective cause such as thrombophlebitis (inflamed painful veins) or a deep vein thrombosis (DVT – swollen, tender, red calf). Seek medical attention.

Hair loss
This is very common and occurs about four months after the birth of your child. Your hair may literally come out in handfuls. This is normal. Some mothers lose hair from temporal areas on the forehead and may even look a little

bald in this area. This too is normal – it will grow back eventually. If you are concerned then have your iron levels and thyroid function checked.

Vitamin D deficiency

This may present in many ways but none are obvious. There are still a lot of unknowns with vitamin D. Vitamin D levels can be measured by a simple blood test. You may have muscle aches and pains or muscle weakness so that getting up from a chair is difficult. To increase vitamin D levels you need to be outside and not covered in anti-UVB sunscreen, which results in blocking the skin making vitamin D (though still avoiding getting sunburnt). Vitamin D can be found in oily fish, eggs, meat and breakfast cereals. It is important to have a good supply of vitamin D when pregnant and when breastfeeding. The National Institute for Health and Clinical Excellence (NICE) suggests that women take 10 micrograms of vitamin D a day during these periods.

If you have dark skin of any tone then you have a higher chance of being vitamin D deficient, especially living in the UK, as you need more sun exposure to make the vitamin D.

Stretch marks

Stretch marks are caused by a combination of genetics, hormonal changes and weight gain. Stretch marks cause breaks in the skins elasticity. They are permanent but they will fade over six months to a year. There are a lot of treatments offered but none are guaranteed to be effective. Laser treatment is not effective if the epidermis and dermis has been affected. Before having any treatment it may be worth discussing your options with your GP.

EMOTIONAL ISSUES

Your emotions can be all over the place when you have a new baby. Your life has changed dramatically, and it can be a lonely time for some of you as you are suddenly at home all the time on your own rather than out with friends or at work surrounded by lots of people. It's likely that you'll have many conflicting emotions as you remember your previous carefree existence and start to realise the day-to-day reality of caring for your baby. Your relationship with your partner will change: you may feel more of a team together and feel closer as you are 'in it together'. But equally, two over-tired people in a house can clash. Your emotions can change from one minute to the next from high to low. You may become snappy, irritable and oversensitive, becoming either defensive or aggressive about anything and everything! You may be feeling vulnerable and a bit lost as you have to learn so much so quickly – it is a very steep learning curve. Or you may not have any of these emotional changes and just take it all in your own stride with a big smile. Try to remember that however you are feeling now, your emotions *will* settle down again. Be kind to yourself and each other and look after yourself as well as your baby.

Bonding

Some of you will bond the first minute you set eyes on your baby, some of you will take longer. It doesn't matter. You will all get it eventually so don't expect fireworks from the start.

In my experience, those who have difficult labours find bonding happens later. Both you and your baby have had a traumatic time. To have some 'post-traumatic stress' would be expected, so be kind to yourself and be patient. Remember to smile to your baby even if you are not quite in the mood. They do copy their parents' faces. It is easy to forget to smile when you are tired and have lots of jobs to do. Keep talking to your baby; if you do not know what to say then try a running commentary of what you have to do or who you are going to see. Singing is also a lot of fun. If you do not know any baby songs then you could learn a few nursery rhymes or songs and have a go – though any music works!

Emotions and breastfeeding

When you are first learning about how to breastfeed you are also just recovering from giving birth and you may be in a bit of shock. You have in your arms this little thing that you have been waiting for for months. Suddenly you may feel overwhelmed, or panic about breastfeeding. What if I cannot breastfeed? What if I fail? Breast is better than formula. It is designed perfectly for your baby. So try and relax and give it a go – you might surprise yourself.

There's no such thing as failure as long as you feed your baby somehow. If your baby struggles to breastfeed and you end up giving it a bottle then you are still doing a great job.

Sleep deprivation

There's no getting away from it: you will be deprived of sleep in the early days – usually the first 8 to 12 weeks, but it can be for longer. Try and take turns to get up at night. If you are breastfeeding then clearly it has to be you who gets up in the night but do not expect your partner to wake up too. One tired person in a house is better than two! Consider one person sleeping in the spare room if you have one.

Relax about getting up at night as your baby does need you for a feed. Easy to say, I know. During the day you have to sleep and rest and whenever possible have help with cooking, cleaning or shopping or taking your baby for a walk. If you are bottle-feeding then possibly take turns at night; if one of you is working then take this into consideration. In the evenings encourage your partner to help you so you do not get too tired. This period of time seems to go on for ages but it is only for a few months before life settles again.

If you are irritable, snappy and low in mood then really try to increase your sleep either by day or by night – it will help. An early night could mean going to bed at 7pm! Also sleep when your baby sleeps during the day, if you can, to get as much rest as possible.

Baby blues

Two-thirds of mums get the baby blues to some extent. It occurs in the first ten days generally and you just burst in to tears for no reason. As a partner, be warned – everything will be going perfectly and then suddenly she will burst into inconsolable tears for no reason. Just give her a cuddle and care for her – it will pass. It is normal, so recognise it and just make sure you have extra rest and good food.

Everyone struggles at some point. The most important thing is **do not take out your frustration on your baby**. Instead, you could try putting your baby in a pushchair and going out – full waterproofs for both of you if it is raining. Put your baby in their cot where your baby is safe, have a cup of coffee and calm yourself down – a short bit of thinking time can help. You could phone a family member, a friend or your partner and ask for help; your health visitor is there to help you, too.

POSTNATAL DEPRESSION

This is **common** and more severe than baby blues. Most lasts three to six months but up to a year is common. Rarely the depression will last for longer. It can start at any time in the first three months after childbirth. It does go eventually so hang in there and do not struggle on alone.

You will be surprised how many other mums have it too or did have it, even though it is not always talked about. At the time everyone is telling you how beautiful your baby is and how lucky you are, underneath you can be feeling flat, low, inadequate and guilty that you just want to hand your baby to someone else and curl up in a ball. You do not want to seem unhappy at what's supposed to be the happiest time of your life. Alternatively you can be in tears all the time and be unable to do anything as you feel totally overwhelmed.

There are lots of emotions occurring – you might feel tired, confused, numb, helpless and hopeless, with negative thoughts such as letting your baby or your family down; that everyone else is coping and you are not; or that no one cares about you. Also, there can be a feeling of distance – not feeling really connected with your baby and everyone around you. Other words to help describe your emotions could be: dark, weary, lost, sad, isolated, unwanted, falling apart, angry, hard, empty, hating, frightened, embarrassed, ridiculous, stupid, bewildered, bitter, mean, and with a heaviness inside and/or empty.

Symptoms of postnatal depression are:

- You will **lose your confidence** and **feel guilty about your baby** and the effect you are having on your baby and everyone around you.

- Depressed people do things they would not ordinarily do such as **yell, shout, snap and react in an explosive manner, be restless or become quiet,** uncommunicative and still.

- You may be **unable to make decisions or to get organised**. Simple things become impossible.

- You may **lose interest** in everything and not have any **concentration** to even watch TV or read a magazine.

- You may have **disturbed sleep** (either insomnia, which is no sleep or poor sleep, or not wanting to wake up and sleep excessively).

- Your **appetite** can also be affected, either going off food or over-eating or drinking more alcohol than you would normally.

- You can also **lose your memory**.

- You may be able to care for your baby really well but at heart you do not want to be involved with your baby.

There is a huge change to your lifestyle when you have a baby. You are no longer in complete control of your life. You need to adapt your life to allow for this little person to come everywhere with you, and however much preparation and planning you make, your baby will dictate what happens next. If you can accept this and go with the flow and not resent or fight the changes that have happened to you, you will find it much easier.

There is a lot of support out there from the health visitor and your GP, and most hospitals have mother and baby units which are a great support haven while you recover.

What can help with postnatal depression:

- **Keep caring for your baby** as much as possible. Keep talking to your baby if you can and use lots of facial expressions as they love that.

- **Get out and about.** Too much time alone gives you too much thinking time, and when depressed this can be very negative and unconstructive. You may not want to but if you are able, try and keep going out.

- **Meet up** with family and friends as much as possible.

- Try to do some **exercise** – it makes a big difference and you always feel better afterwards. It is just getting started that's the hurdle.

- Eat a **healthy diet**. Try to avoid too much processed sugar, processed fat and chocolate. Keep your alcohol consumption low – maximum a small glass a night. Alcohol can have a negative effect with depression – you think it will make you feel better but you end up waking up more tired in the morning then feeling even more overwhelmed and then more depressed.

- **Rest** as much as possible – do not try to do too much in a day. If the housework does not get done it does not matter. Get others to help you if you are not managing. Babies are exhausting – they need so much care and you are not getting your usual 7-9 hours sleep a night and you may be breastfeeding as well as recovering from your pregnancy and labour, so you need to recuperate. Be kind to yourself, set your aims low and rest.

- **Tell your husband or partner** – get him involved. You may not want to talk or even be able to explain yourself but at least say that you are struggling or show him this page. You will probably already be behaving irrationally, not being very warm and avoiding contact. It will give him a purpose and help explain your behaviour, which will be upsetting. He may even get depressed or be depressed too.

- **Tell your friends** – it will help explain your behaviour such as a lack of a smile and enthusiasm for your baby.

- **Ask for help** – the depression will pass and it will be more fulfilling and positive if those around you know how you feel. You may even find others who have been through the same. Do not be ashamed; do not become isolated, aloof or withdrawn. Your family and friends will want to support you and they can if they understand how you are feeling.

- **Keep believing that you will get better** because you will. Your feelings will improve with time.

- Take **multivitamins and multiminerals** supplements to help build yourself back up.

- **Avoid hormonal contraception** until you are better as it can add to your low mood.

- **Do not self-criticise** – try to focus on the positives.

- To help yourself get things done, **write lists** of things you want to do and start at the top. Even if you only do one thing a day, by the end of a week you will have achieved a lot.

- **Try a thought diary** – you write down the event or problem, then you write down your thoughts and feelings, then try writing down what your thoughts would be if you were not depressed. Such as: my baby cries when I put him in his cot. **Thoughts may be** – I am a useless mother, no one else's baby does this, I cannot bear the crying, what am I doing wrong, nothing seems to work for me, I cannot cope with this any longer. **Feelings** – depressed, guilty, failure, loss of self-confidence. **What would I be thinking if I was not depressed?** My baby is fine, gaining weight, he has had enough food today, he may be a bit over-tired but has had enough sleep today, his nappy is clean, he is winded, he is not hungry so he is fine to leave and have a little cry. He needs to settle himself so he can learn to go to sleep easily as he gets older. Also I **am being a good mother**.

- **Keep a compliment diary** or achievement notebook, as when you are depressed you are unable to remember anything positive. Write these down, for example: Amanda said I looked good today; my health visitor said my baby was really thriving. Whatever means something to you – that is what matters.

- **Cognitive behavioural therapy** (CBT) works well. You can access this online for free now. Counselling can also help as a lot of previous personal problems can sometimes return at this time.

If you have severe depression then **antidepressants** do work, and you can take them when breastfeeding. It is sometimes better to treat your severe depression than to struggle on without medication. Antidepressants are not addictive; if you do need them, think you will be on them for a minimum of six months and then see how you feel. Do not stop the antidepressants until you feel well again and do **not** stop them suddenly.

In some areas there are groups for mums with postnatal depression – ask your health visitor if there any locally or look online; '1BIGdatabase' for your area can have a lot of local information and see if there is a group for you to join.

Puerperal Psychosis is a <u>very rare</u> severe medical condition where the mother hears voices, behaves oddly, is paranoid, irrational and often has no insight to her problem. The mother is a risk to herself and her baby. If this happens to you, others around you will diagnose it and you will need to go into hospital for treatment.

ADJUSTING TO BEING AT HOME
Some of you will love being at home caring for your baby and others will find it very difficult. The first few weeks will be quiet while you get to know your new baby. Here are some ideas to help you through the transition if you are finding it difficult – try gradually introducing some of these ideas as your confidence grows:

• **Try to go out with your baby once a day**, regardless of the weather. If it is freezing outside you may not be able to. You will feel so much better afterwards even if the thought of bothering seems too much. Your baby will also sleep better. If you go for walks at their sleep times the motion of the buggy/pram can make them fall asleep alternatively go for a walk after their sleep so you can get the rest you need too.

• **Go to the same café** either with someone or by yourself. If you go to the same place the owner will get to know you and you will create a place to go. Other customers will often stop to 'coo' at your baby: people love babies and often stop to chat, which will give you an outside contact and some self-esteem. Perhaps meet up with a friend or with someone from your antenatal group. It makes it more fun and your days don't feel so long. Try to make the effort, however tired you are, with the other new mothers as it is good to have someone to discuss your baby issues with.

- If you have the inclination/budget then try and find a **gym with a crèche,** or ask someone to look after your baby for an hour each week on a regular basis; you could take turns with another mum. There are also mums and babies Pilates/yoga classes and buggy fitness groups that will help you to meet other people at the same stage as you as well as get some exercise.

- Join or create **a book club** – this is a great excuse to meet up with other mums or dads and talk about non-baby issues. This does pre-suppose that you have time to read a whole book! If you're in the right group, it won't matter either way.

- **Shorten the weekly shop**. Supermarkets can take a long time which may become stressful if your baby starts screaming. Alternatively shop on line for the bulky items and then go to the butcher, baker, grocer and smaller supermarkets. This gives you a purpose to getting out, keeps your baby entertained and allows you the opportunity to stop for feeding, changing and a coffee. Also it is a fantastic opportunity to get the local gossip and gives you other things to talk about.

- Try out your **local mums and baby groups**. See if you can **help in some way** even if it is making the tea as this can sometimes make conversation easier if you have a purpose. The odds are that you'll find at least one person you get on with.

- Try to see the **cultural things in your area** such as art galleries or national monuments. If they are free you won't mind leaving after five minutes if your baby is crying.

- Go online to meet a mum at www.mama.co.uk if there is one in your area, or create your own meet a mum club. Also look at www.1bigdatabase.org.uk for more information about your local area.

- **Learn new recipes** and reward yourself and your partner with a delicious supper once a week. You are going to be in most of the nights anyway. This will be good for your relationship and may give you a great sense of satisfaction.

The most important thing is to really adjust your standards and expectations, and feel that anything you can achieve is a triumph!

Meeting other mothers

If you were part of an antenatal group, you may have met some other mothers you got on with. Texting is a good way to communicate with each other if you are worried about phoning at the wrong time.

Do go to baby groups and try to chat to the other mums. Often you don't feel like it – many of us resist the idea of making new friends. Give it a go. The other mothers have just the same feelings and anxieties as you have, and it can be surprisingly helpful and reassuring to meet people who are in the same boat as you. If you are really stuck for conversation then try complimenting their baby's clothes or ask how the pushchair works and find out where they bought it from.

To find out about different groups your health visitors can be helpful. Also look online, look in the local magazine/newspaper/books on your locality or find out what happens each week in the church hall. There are also lots of mums' groups on the internet which can be an easy way to share any worries.

Going back to work

This is not always an easy decision. Some of you will want to get back to work, others will have no choice and others still may struggle to decide what's best. The bottom line is that you will not know how you feel until you have had your baby. Write down your reasons for and against going back to work.

Look at the many options for childcare, from grandparents, if they are keen, to childminders, nannies, nursery and crèches. Take your time to decide, look around and compare the cost of each option. Talk to other parents about their experiences so you feel fully informed. Also think ahead as some of your options may get booked up early.

It is not an easy time as you have the stress of remembering your job again and also concern that your child is being well looked after. It is a juggling act but it can all work out.

For legal and financial advice go to:

www.hse.gov.uk/mothers or www.dwp.gov.uk

Other web sites:

www.familyinformationservices.org.uk (FIS) - which is linked to your local authority.

4: FATHERS, COUPLES, SINGLE PARENTS

FATHERS

Congratulations on being a father! Your involvement in your baby's care from the day they are born is so good for your child's emotional and educational development. Your presence and kindness also has a great effect on your child's self-esteem and inner confidence. Your child needs a father as much as a mother.

No one knows how they are going to feel about their new son or daughter until he/she is born. Some of you will be besotted; others will go into panic mode about the responsibilities that lie ahead; some may even resent the new baby for getting in the way of your lifestyle and forcing you to share your partner's affection. The emotional experience of having a baby may affect you in some way. **Postnatal depression** in fathers is common but not often talked about, and the chapter on postnatal depression applies as much to you as your partner. Be kind to yourself and give yourself time to adjust to your new role. **Bonding** is just as variable – some of you will bond instantly, while for others it will happen later. Give it all time.

Your participation, encouragement and support will have an important influence on your partner's experience. Your baby will affect each of you and your relationship, in both positive and negative ways. There will be times when your partner will be totally exhausted and strung-out, and you may never have seen her like this before. **Try to not argue, to not criticise, and to be as supportive as possible. This is a phase and it will pass.**

If you want to get the most out of this phase of your life, keep yourself healthy and fit. Get involved with the care of your baby. Some dads find it hard to find a role and feel useful in the very early days, especially if the mother is breastfeeding. But maybe bath-time will be your thing, or winding the baby and settling them when they are fed. You can have them lying or sitting near you if you have a job to do and chat to them. Initially you may feel uncertain, worry you may hurt the baby and it may all feel difficult and fiddly. So take your time, go slowly – the more you do it, the easier it gets.

Try not to get frustrated if you can't think of a logical solution to each problem. There is not always a rational explanation for a baby's behaviour. Children have no sense until they are at least three years old so aim to keep them away from trouble rather than expecting your baby to learn from its mistakes.

Remember to be careful when swinging them by their hands as they can easily dislocate their elbow joint, look above your head first if you lift them up high and be careful of their little legs when using a highchair that goes under the table.

Supporting the new mum

New mums may be feeling fat, flabby, unattractive and grey-eyed. It is not for long but at this time they need lots of extra love and care. They may not be in need of much more! Have a laugh at your own expense about the lack of sex and try not to demand any. If you play your cards right you will be rewarded in time. Also if you make sure your partner has more rest they may have more energy....

Your partner may be more emotionally sensitive than usual and any useful advice or criticism may be taken the wrong way so tread carefully. They may also snap at you for no reason so stay calm and try not to take it personally. Mistakes are normal and all part of the learning curve you are both on. Never assume anything of your partner, always ask what they would like first. **Keep talking and keep communicating**.

If you join in the care of your baby, you will work better as a team and you will enjoy it all more. In the early days you are mainly aiming to survive the sleep deprivation; go for a walk, do bath-time and change the odd nappy – alongside the shopping, cooking and cleaning. Caring for a newborn can be a full-time job, mainly because it takes so long to feed and wind them. If your partner has done nothing all day, do not be surprised! You may get the complete lowdown on the day when you return from work; she may not have talked to anyone that day. Try and be a good listener; the days will get more interesting as your baby gets older.

Be warned you may return from work at the end of a day and handed a baby as you walk through the door by a partner who needs a bit of time out. If you start feeling resentful, **try looking after your baby for a day**. I appreciate that is difficult if your partner is breastfeeding. But caring for your child will give you more of an understanding of your partner's situation – the limitations, time constraints and planning needed to care for such a small thing.

You can really help in lots of practical ways: for example,encourage your partner to **take a break** – have a rest, a bath or go for a walk.

You may also need a break so talk to each other and agree a plan. Your sleep will also be disturbed, weekends will change and lie-ins are likely to become a fond distant memory.

There will be less time to exercise but keep doing something to keep yourself fit. It is just a phase of life but if you look after yourself you will find rewards in different ways.

If you are a stay-at-home dad, have a look at

www.homedad.org.uk as well as

www.1bigdatabase.org.uk.

CARING FOR YOUR RELATIONSHIP

You have gone from a carefree couple to parenthood overnight. The impact will be different for every couple, but at the very least you are going to get less sleep and less time to yourselves. If you can work together to get as much sleep as possible, to get some time to yourself and some time as a couple, you are far more likely to enjoy this phase of your life together.

Avoid the 'competitive exhaustion syndrome' where both of you stay up during the evenings and nights – you will both be exhausted. It can take some mothers a couple of years to totally recover physically from childbirth, while some fathers take longer to mentally adjust to their new role. Due to this level of emotions and tiredness, one or both of you may become very sensitive and advice and criticism can easily be interpreted the wrong way, so tread carefully and look after each other. Also avoid the 'competitive parenting' you are both needed to bring up your child even if at times it may not feel like it.

You love each other but you now have to divide your love, time and attention to another. Relationships work best at this time when you are both involved. Don't be over-protective with your baby and share the experience.

Working as a team

- Look out for each other as you will experience **extreme tiredness.**
- Consider **working in shifts** – so you are not both awake at two in the morning. Have alternate lie-ins at the weekend.
- **Keep communicating** – television, telephones, books and computers can be harmful to relationships if over-used!
- **Keep your conversation varied** – not just on the topic of children.
- **Resolve conflicts** before you go to sleep that night.
- **Enjoy your nights in together** – as there will be more of them! Enjoy being intimate together and just hanging out together. Give your relationship as much time and thought as possible even when you are extremely tired.
- If you have a late night, drink **less alcohol** – you no longer get the undisturbed sleep or lie-ins in order to recover.
- **Share the domestic workload** – babies create a huge amount of washing.
- **Share the baby care** – feeding (if bottle-fed), bathing, nappies and walks. You are both responsible for the care of your baby and there will be times in your lives when this can be stressful. Share the good times and the difficult times.
- **Talk about finances so there are no nasty surprises.** Disagreement about money is of the biggest causes of divorce. Work as a team, especially if one of you has given up your job to look after the baby. When you are at home all the time it is easier to spend money than when you are busy at work.

Equally babies do cost more to have around so there is less extra money than you are used to. Budgets are effective and can help you both plan your expenses fairly.

- Keep **exercising** – this is not as easy as it was before your baby arrived. This is an easy time to gain weight but a difficult time to lose it.
- If your family or friends offer to look after your baby so you can **go out** together then grab the opportunity, even if it is just for a short time.
- Be careful not to lose touch with your friends.
- Other family members may get involved – some are wonderful, some are more challenging. Remember these are long-term relationships and most of your issues of the moment will disappear in time.
- Your expectations of being a family, parenting, your future together may all change so **keep an open mind and keep talking.**
- If you **feel vulnerable** due to your new responsibility, keep talking so those around you can understand your change in behaviour. Do not think you are alone if you are perpetually tired, grumpy, moody and/or irritable.
- **More planning** is needed to do things. You not only have to get yourself dressed and out, you have your baby too – with the nappies, bottles, change of clothes, etc....

Nurture your relationship

Give your partner/husband some attention and also compliment him when he is with your baby. Let him have lots of cuddles from you and your baby. Do not take love for granted, it needs encouragement and appreciation. Keep talking and keep cuddling and kissing even if you do not want to be more intimate. Have some time in the evening together or try and do things you did before your baby arrived together.

It is important to work on your relationship even when you are constantly tired. If men feel unwanted, unloved or unneeded, they can start to feel deserted and depressed and may drift away. Not all men are great communicators so you may not realise until the damage is done to your relationship. Sadly this is the highest time for divorce, especially when the baby is 0-2 years old.

SINGLE PARENTS

There are lots of positives bringing up a child on your own and you will be rewarded and have a lot of fun. You are not on your own – about one in ten children are brought up by a single parent.

Do not be afraid to ask for help and advice as there is a lot to learn about bringing up a baby and the emotional changes and challenges you will have.

The following suggestions might help:

• It will be hard at times so try and **build a good network** of family and friends around you. Use all the support networks available – your heath visitor will be a good local resource. Internet sites like www.gingerbread.org.uk (0800 018 5026) or www.onespace.org.uk can give you some financial or legal advice and it has a good A-Z list of useful organisations including holiday ideas. It is also a site to help young mums. www.1bigdatabase.org.uk is another internet site to tell you about all the support groups and societies in your area.

• The most important thing to do is to **look after yourself**. Keep yourself fit, eat healthily and try to stay mentally strong. Focus on the positives and try to look at problems as challenges.

• **Trust your instinct**, listen to advice then use the advice that works for you.

• **Stay positive** and encouraging with your baby.

• **Share your feelings and be honest**. Talk about your fears or worries if you have them. **Postnatal depression** is as common for the single parent as the married parent.

• Try and **find time for yourself**, accept all help to look after your child so you can go out and keep in touch with your friends.

Look at this web site:

www.familyinformationservices.org.uk (FIS)
- which is linked to your local authority.

5: MEDICAL INFORMATION

The following information is to help you not scare you. It is not a replacement for medical advice. I have mentioned the common medical problems only.

Normal body temperature = 36°C to 37°C or 96.8°F to 98.4°F

SERIOUS ILLNESS

If your baby is unwell, seek urgent medical advice early. If your baby has **any** of the following symptoms they may have a serious illness:

- A **high-pitched or weak cry**, continuous cry, **less responsive** than normal, less active or more **floppy** than usual.

- **Mottled-looking cold hands and feet <u>and a high temperature</u>** (above 38°C or 100.4°F)

- A **non-blanching rash**: especially with purple spots that are bigger than 0.2cm. If you press your finger on part of the rash it should go back to normal skin colour but if it stays purple, like a deep bruise, then that is a non-blanching rash and needs attention.

- Pale skin, **grunting** when breathing, **flaring their nostrils** when breathing and/or **using their tummy and ribs to breathe**. **Blue/grey colour** around their mouth.

• **Passing less urine** – nappies not as heavy or just dry.

• **Vomiting pure green fluid** – very rarely the bowel can become twisted. This needs urgent surgical treatment.

• Passing **clots of blood in the stool**.

• **High fever** – above 38°C if under three months or above 39°C if over three months. Sweating a lot.

• **Stiff neck/body** – i.e. Not able to put their head on their chest and holding their head very still.

VERY URGENT MEDICAL ADVICE is needed if your baby stops breathing or goes blue, has a fit, is unresponsive, has a glazed look or cannot be woken from sleep.

Other signs that your baby is not well include going off food, refusing to eat or drink fluids, wanting to be held all the time, lethargic or just being irritable.

FIRST AID KIT

Have the following in your house at all times (out of reach of all children):

• **Plasters** and **scissors**
• **Tweezers** – for splinters
• **Antiseptic cream**
• **Antihistamine cream**
• Something for **insect stings**
• **Thermometer** – ask you pharmacist. The ear ones are easy to use and reliable.

- **Paracetamol** for infants – for all pains and fevers. It is safe for all infants but do not exceed the recommended dose and only give when really needed. If you want more pain control please seek medical advice. Writing down when you gave the last dose can help avoid prescribing errors.
- **NSAIDs (anti-inflammatory medication** – please ask your pharmacist if you are unsure) for infants it is good for pains and fevers. Do not exceed the recommended dose and write down when it was last given.
- **Oral antihistamine** for infants – this is great for sudden itchy rashes, insect bites, allergic rashes or reactions. Some can make your child very drowsy whilst others can make you child hyperactive; every child is different.
- **Arnica** for bruises – it is amazing how quickly a child will stop crying when they have hurt themselves and are offered some cream! Arnica can relieve the pain and extent of the bruise if you rub it in and re-apply regularly.
- **Burns spray**
- **Vinegar** for wasp stings and jelly fish stings
- **Vaseline** is excellent for their face in the cold and wind to prevent it going red. Also for ticks: smother it on (butter also works) – it stops the ticks breathing so the tick lets go, though it may take a while. Try to avoid ripping the tick out or you may leave the head in which can be very irritating.
- **Ice** in the freezer. Great for insect stings; also sucking on an ice cube can decrease swelling in the mouth but watch out for choking.
- **Aloe Vera** - Good for sunburn, scars and non-healing scars as it stops your child scratching the scar and also helps healing.

MEDICAL A-Z

BOWELS
Constipation

Constipation is when your baby has not passed stool for up to 5 days if breastfeeding or up to 3 days if bottle feeding or is passing very hard stool which is painful.

If your baby is constipated and taking formula/bottle then first of all add an ounce of extra water to the formula. You are thereby diluting the feed but not decreasing the amount of formula in each feed.

Once you are giving your baby food, constipation can be relieved by including the following in their diet: stewed apple or apple juice, orange juice, prune juice (a tin of prunes in their juice, not syrup – blend it and give about a teaspoon to a tablespoon at a time depending on the size/age of your baby or the effect of the prunes), linseed oil, kiwi and pawpaw. Bananas can either help constipation or cause it.

If extra water or foods make no difference to the constipation then see your doctor. Sometimes a regular laxative is useful.

Baby massage or craniosacral osteopathy can also be very effective for some babies.

Diarrhoea and/or vomiting

Diarrhoea can last from one to 14 days although most has stopped by day 5. Vomiting usually lasts up to three days. Sudden-onset diarrhoea and or vomiting may be due to an infection otherwise known as **gastroenteritis**. Most babies with gastroenteritis do not need medical treatment unless they become dehydrated.

If they become dehydrated they become restless and clingy with sunken eyes and a sunken fontanelle (the soft area on the head just above the forehead), a dry mouth and dry, cold skin. Their feet may also be mottled or pale. They may have stopped passing urine so their nappies are dry; sometimes this can be difficult to spot if they also have diarrhoea. This can happen very quickly especially when they are very small. Your baby may need medical help however most can be treated at home.

If they become **floppy and less responsive** they need medical help.

Contact your doctor:

- If the diarrhoea has been going on for longer than 2-3 days
- If there is blood in the diarrhoea
- If your baby is not able to keep any fluids down and has not passed urine
- If your baby becomes drowsy or confused
- If your baby has a high temperature − this is defined as above 38°C if under three months or above 39°C if over three months.
- If your baby has returned from foreign travel
- If your baby is breathing quickly or with difficulty
- If your baby's tummy is painful when you touch it
- If your baby has cold, pale or mottled feet.

If your baby is under 1 year old, be more vigilant as they can become very unwell very quickly.

If you are completely breastfeeding then keep going. Increase the number of times you feed in a day: try to give them feeds little and often. You can also top them up with cooled boiled water and/or rehydration fluids (from your pharmacist). You may find a syringe or a teaspoon helps to get the fluid in.

If you are bottle/formula feeding then you can keep giving them formula but, again, give it little and often. If the diarrhoea and vomiting is not settling then stop the formula for 12-24 hours or so and give them rehydration fluids or cooled boiled water. Give them 1oz or 30ml frequently but never the whole bottle: it will just come straight back up. 'Frequently' means about every 15 to 30 minutes depending on how much they can take at one time.

If your baby vomits, do not give them anything at all for an hour or so then give them 10mls of water. Then wait for 30 minutes and if that stays down then give them 30mls (1oz) every 30 minutes, increasing to every 15 minutes as your baby improves. If that stays down, increase the amount you are giving them to 60ml (2oz) each time. Slowly increase the volume if they continue to not vomit. If they start vomiting again then stop and start again, with no fluids for an hour. If your baby is vomiting a lot, do not give milk or food for at least six to 12 hours after the last vomit. If you are at all concerned discuss it with your doctor. Build up slowly with foods, starting with very simple foods – such as banana, dry toast, rice and boiled vegetables – and very small amounts. Avoid fruit juice until your baby is well again. Babies and young children should never be given carbonated drinks.

If your baby has diarrhoea, follow the same fluid instructions as for sickness. If you are bottle-feeding and the diarrhoea stopped and then the diarrhoea restarts when you give your baby milk again, the diarrhoea may be due to a lactose intolerance which is common after an episode of gastroenteritis. Sometimes babies and young children can get short-term lactose intolerance for a few weeks. Either put up with diarrhoea every day until it settles, or give them lactose-free formula or milk and every week or so introduce dairy again. Most lactose-intolerance settles within six weeks and then you can return to the standard formula or dairy.

Other causes of vomiting:

Vomiting can also be caused by **other infections**, such as: tonsillitis, ear infection, appendicitis and urinary tract infection (bladder infection).

Non-infective causes of vomiting include:

- Congenital – some babies just vomit as a result of an under-developed oesophagus which they all grow out of in time and therefore needs no medical intervention. Thickening the feeds can sometimes help.
- Reflux
- Food allergy – especially cow's milk and/or soya
- Malrotation of the bowel – causing green vomit (bile-stained vomit)
- Behavioural
- Other rarer causes for your doctor to assess and diagnose.

Other causes of diarrhoea:

- Certain foods or too much of one food, for example apple juice, mango juice or apricots.
- Inflammation in the intestines
- Malabsorbtion – the stool is often offensive-smelling, pale, bulky and floats in the toilet so is difficult to flush.

Some children have chronic diarrhoea or vomiting for no known reason and as long as they are gaining weight and growing there is usually not a serious underlying cause.

If your child has diarrhoea or vomiting, always wash your hands and everyone else's hands in the household to prevent spread of the infection. Do this especially before preparing and eating food. Clean the toilet, taps and door handles often with disinfectant. Your child should not go back to any childcare facility for 48 hours after the last episode of diarrhoea or vomiting and not swim in a public pool for two weeks.

CHICKENPOX   (*Herpes Zoster*)

When someone is infectious with chickenpox, they can pass it on to the next person from two days before the rash appears until after the last blister dries up. To catch chickenpox you probably need to be in the same room as an infected person for about 15 minutes or face to face with them for about five minutes. You can only have shingles – the rash – if you have had chickenpox at some time in your past. You can catch chickenpox from shingles if you have not had chickenpox before and therefore are not immune. If the shingles rash is under clothing it would be very hard to get chickenpox from it.

If you have had chickenpox then you are immune, and you pass this protection on to your baby. If anyone with chickenpox is in contact with your baby within the first seven days after birth your baby will be protected by your immune system. If you then breastfeed, this immunity continues until you stop breastfeeding.

If you have not had chickenpox and therefore are not immune to it neither is your baby. If your baby is in contact with chickenpox within the first seven days of birth he/she will need an injection of VZIG which is given by your doctor. The sooner it is given the more effective it is; ideally it is given within ten days of contact with chickenpox.

COUGHS

There are many types of coughs out there and the best way to prevent spread of infection is through hand washing.

Coughs and Colds or Viral Respiratory Tract Infections

There are a lot of cold viruses about and children need to build up their immunity to them. Children can get many colds in a year, especially when they first start nursery or playgroups. Cold viruses like cold weather, so the colder it is or the colder you are, the more likely you are to be infected.

Viral colds often have a dry cough with or without a fever. Your child may have shivers or feel cold and your child may be sleepy or tired.

If your child has a cold, keep them at home. Paracetamol may help make your child more comfortable, although there is evidence that the fever helps clear the infection. Your child may be off their food, which is fine, but encourage fluids such as water or continue breastfeeding or bottle feeding. Some other things that may help include

- Gently patting their backs in coughing fits.
- Unblocking their nose to feed using a suction bulb.
- Nasal saline drops – either from the pharmacist or $1/8^{th}$ of a teaspoon of salt in 100ml cooled boiled water – put 2-3 drops in each nostril then wait 5-10 minutes before using a nasal suction bulb.
- Vapour rubs – from the pharmacist.
- Humidification – either sitting in a steamy bathroom, or a cold-mist humidifier or a steam vaporiser or simply putting a bowel of hot water on the radiator. Make sure anything hot is out of reach from your baby or any toddler.
- Raise the legs of their cot at the head end by about 10cms off the floor to help them breathe more easily when asleep.
- Keeping their ears warm when out on a cold day.

If your child has a cough and is losing weight then it is important to see your doctor.

Some specific lung conditions are:

Bacterial Chest Infections

The best signs for bacterial chest infections are a persistent fever and fast breathing with or without a cough. They may also be floppy or lethargic, off food and generally unwell. Antibiotics are needed.

Viral Lower Respiratory Tract Infection

This describes a viral infection that affects the larger parts of the lungs. It starts with a dry cough which then becomes productive (i.e. your child coughs up mucous) after a few days and may have a mild temperature. Your child may sound like they have an 'older person's' cough, but their chest is actually clear. The cough will clear with time and generally does not need medicine. It may trigger an asthma attack if your child becomes wheezy, or it may have a bacterial infection as well which will need antibiotics.

Bronchiolitis or Viral Induced Wheeze

Bronchiolitis or viral induced wheeze is an inflammation of the smaller parts of the lungs caused by a virus. It is bronchiolitis if your child is less than one year, and viral induced wheeze if your child is older than one year. It usually requires no treatment but the symptoms are very distressing. Very occasionally hospital treatment is needed.

It starts with a cough, runny nose and mild fever. After a few days the cough becomes worse, wheezing starts and the rate of breathing increases. Occasionally in more serious cases babies can turn blue, especially around their mouth, use their ribs to breathe (so the skin between the ribs goes inwards when they breathe) and have a fever. It is important to keep your child well-hydrated. **Seek urgent medical help if your child is vomiting, refusing to feed, breathing rapidly, using its ribs to breathe and has to sit up to breathe.**

The wheeze usually lasts for three to five days; the cough may last a few weeks. Many children who have had bronchiolitis will wheeze again with the next cold. Most will grow out of the wheeze.

Croup

Croup can start between the ages of six months and three years. It is a 'barking' noise when breathing in, accompanied by a runny nose and a temperature. Your child may sound like a seal! It is generally worse at night and lasts about two to seven days. It is viral and most croup does not need treatment. Urgent medical treatment is needed if your child is struggling to breathe, turning blue-grey around their mouth and drowsy. Steroids are very effective if needed. Stay calm and try to calm your child down (watching TV or reading a book might help) this can really help their breathing. Sit your child upright; fresh air or a steamy room can also help. If your child has had croup once he/she will be more likely to get it again.

Whooping cough (Pertussis)

Bordatella Pertussis causes whooping cough, otherwise known as the 100 day cough. It mainly affects the unimmunised. It presents as a mild cough for one to two weeks then turns to a 'whoop' type of cough that can trigger endless fits of coughing. When severe the coughing fits can cause a lack of oxygen to the brain (hypoxia) and your child can turn blue, especially around the mouth (cyanosis), or have a pressure effect on the brain. It is highly contagious and can be very serious for babies under a year old. Some children may not have a 'whoop' but may just have small episodes of stopping breathing for short periods. It is a bacterial infection; however antibiotics can only stop it spreading to other children and adults – but antibiotics do not affect the course of the Pertussis.

Cystic Fibrosis

CF is a genetic disorder affecting the lungs and digestive system. Most are now diagnosed at the newborn screen. It affects the lungs making it difficult to clear the mucous so breathing can be difficult and chest infections and coughs are very common. It also affects the digestive system. The thick mucous blocks the enzymes needed to break down food, so diarrhoea and poor weight gain are common problems.

EARS

A child with an ear infection can be irritable, vomiting, restless, screaming, off their food, with a high temperature and possibly, but not necessarily, tugging on the ear affected. It is generally recommended to wait 48 hours before giving antibiotics as a large percentage clear up within this time. During this first 48 hours, unless they are severely ill, try paracetamol and NSAIDs (anti-inflammatory medication) from your pharmacist. Also a warm compress may help using a flannel dipped in warm water or a warm (not hot) hot-water bottle wrapped in a towel. Leave it on for 10-15 minutes at a time.

EYES

Blocked tear duct
This is when there is creamy yellow discharge in the corner of the eye near the nose and it is due to the tube between the eye and nose not being properly open. It may look like conjunctivitis or an eye infection. It may be worth asking your doctor to swab it and check it is not an infection. The eye itself is not red. The discharge can be continually present. It usually sorts itself out by six months to a year. After a year a small operation to open the tube (the lacrimal duct) may be appropriate. Large 'crocodile' tears will be normal until it clears. It can get worse when your baby has a cold. To clean it, ideally use cooled boiled water and a small cotton wool ball. A clean tissue can be just as effective.

Conjunctivitis

Conjunctivitis is when the eye itself is red and there is a sticky discharge in the eye. It is now regarded as self-limiting so generally antibiotics are not needed unless it is very red with lots of discharge. You will need antibiotics if your baby is attending nursery as it can be very contagious and easily passed with little fingers.

Red Eye

If the whole eye is red and swollen including the skin around the eye you need to see your doctor.

Squint

A squint is when the eyeballs do not move together, so with certain movements the eyes are in different places in the eye. This can be normal when they are first born as the muscles are developing. If this occurs only when tired then they are generally ok. If this is present all the time then you need to be referred to an eye specialist.

FEBRILE CONVULSIONS

This is a fit or seizure that is triggered by a rapid rise in temperature. Most children are aged six months to six years. It is most common when they are 2 years old. Often your child has been unwell and has a temperature. The convulsion lasts from a few seconds to ten minutes. Your child will suddenly turn blue, go rigid and stare and may have shaking arms and legs. It is a very frightening experience and you will need urgent medical help. If it is a recurrent event then you can learn how to treat your child at home.

If your baby does have a fit then make sure the area around them is safe and do not put anything, including medicine, into their mouth. Once the fit has stopped, lie your baby down on its side and tummy, head slightly extended, or stretch the neck gently and have the face tilted to the ground or floor. This is in case they vomit; if their face is towards the floor then the vomit runs out of their mouth. If your child is hot then cool them down – open windows, switch off the heating and take their clothes off if you can. Paracetamol helps – they can be given as suppositories. Do not give your baby anything orally (into their mouth) until he/she is alert again. Sometimes antibiotics are needed to treat the underlying illness.

GENITALS

Breast enlargement and vaginal discharge
Both boys and girls can present with breast tissue when born, sometimes it is only on one side. The breasts can also release a little fluid when only a few days old. This is due to the mother's hormones, and will settle. The same is true for a very small vaginal bleed or mucous discharge in baby girls.

Undescended testes
Both testes should be felt in the scrotal sacs by two weeks of age. It is important for them to be examined again at the six-week check. Most testes descend into the scrotal sac by six months. If one or both testes have not descended by this time then a surgical paediatric opinion is needed. A small operation may be needed to bring the testes down into the scrotal sac when your boy is about a year old. This is now not checked after the '6 week check' so look yourself and it you are unsure ask you GP to examine.

Circumcision and the foreskin
For some religions **circumcision** is normal. It is otherwise done if medically necessary. Make sure the person doing the circumcision is qualified and it is done in a very clean environment to avoid infection. If the penis looks an odd shape or the urinary meatus (the hole, to pass urine out of) is not at the end then you should delay a circumcision and seek medical advice first. The condition is called

hypospadias – the foreskin is needed for the reconstruction of the penis so your son can pass urine in a straight line when he is older. This is a rare problem but important to check for.

The **foreskin** does not retract until your son is about three or four years old.

HEAD SHAPE AND TORTICOLLIS

An odd head shape is either due to plagiocephaly (flat head syndrome) which is very common and harmless, or a very rare condition called craniosynostosis, which is where the bones in the head fuse too early and needs urgent medical attention.

Plagiocephaly is the most common cause: the head is asymmetrical due to the positioning in the uterus and following delivery. Most babies' heads look odd when first born then develop into a more normal shape after a few weeks. A caesarean section does not prevent having an odd head shape.

If the head shape is odd due to always sleeping on one side, it is called positional plagiocephaly, and mainly occurs in the first three months. Put your baby in its cot the other way round. To look to the light, your baby has to turn its head the other way. When your baby is asleep you can try turning the head or putting a little rolled-up towel to encourage the head to rest at a different angle. Always put your baby to sleep on its back looking up at you. Also play on either side of your baby. Tummy time when awake will also help reshape their heads and help develop neck and trunk strength. Most odd head shapes are covered by hair when older and not noticeable.

A **torticollis** can also affect the head shape; this is a muscle spasm that causes the head to tilt to one side or only turn in one direction.

Specialised physiotherapy can help plagiocephaly and torticollis. Some parents have found craniosacral osteopathy or cranial orthosis effective but neither is evidence based. After eight months these treatments will be less effective.

HEART

Heart murmurs are listened for when first born, at the paediatric examination and at the six-week check. Some murmurs are harmless and others need medical treatment. If your baby has a heart problem then he/she may turn blue around the mouth and/or fingers and toes when feeding or crying. Your child may be breathless when feeding or crying. Other symptoms are having a fast breathing rate, sweating, poor feeding and failure to thrive. If you are at all concerned see your doctor.

HERNIAS

Hernias are caused by the abdominal lining or a small section of bowel being pushed through a weak spot in the abdominal wall.

Inguinal Hernias are small swellings in the groin area, under the nappy. These can cause a lot of pain and do need surgery sometimes urgently if the hernia obstructs and blocks the bowel. Inguinal hernias are more common in premature babies and boys.

Umbilical Hernias are swellings that come out of the umbilicus/tummy button. Most will disappear within a year; the rest by the age of five.

Para-umbilical Hernias are swellings or hernias that appear near the umbilicus/tummy button. These are different and may need surgery.

HIPS

Occasionally the hips do not form completely so the socket is flat. If this is treated early they can return to normal, so all babies have their hips checked: the doctors are looking out for a 'click' in the hips, different leg lengths and limited movement. An ultrasound scan can always be done if there are any concerns or if there is a family history of congenital hip problems.

KNEES AND FEET

Knocked knees or bow legs generally sort themselves out. However it may be worth checking with your doctor to see if your baby has a vitamin D deficiency. Talipes, or fixed deformity of the feet, will need medical intervention. Feet that are turned in or out generally straighten with time. Please see your doctor if you are concerned.

MENINGITIS

Meningitis is an infection of one of the layers which covers the brain and spinal cord. The infection causes the layer to swell and this puts pressure on the brain and nerves, which can be damaged. It can be caused by a bacteria or a virus.

There are **early warning signs** which include **having a fever** with either:

- **Severe pains in their legs or hands**
- **Unusually cold hands or feet**
- **Pale skin and blue lips**.

Other signs include being floppy, unresponsive, an unusual high-pitched cry, vomiting, refusing feeds, blotchy skin and a vacant staring expression. **A rash may not always be present.** The other symptoms of headache, stiff neck, drowsiness, seizures and light sensitivity with a fever are not generally seen in young children.

If you are at all concerned please seek urgent medical advice. If the symptoms begin suddenly and then rapidly worsen phone 999 immediately and ask for an ambulance.

NOSE

Babies use their nose to breathe through so they can feed and breathe at the same time. Therefore, if they have a cold and have a blocked nose they will not feed well. Saline nasal drops from a pharmacist or 1/8th of a teaspoon of salt in 100ml cooled boiled water – put 2-3 drops in each nostril then wait 5-10 minutes before using a nasal suction bulb can be very effective at clearing the nose for the time it takes to feed. You may only need to use a nasal pipette/suction bulb to suck the nasal discharge out. If your baby has a blocked nose raise the head end of their cot by putting large books or bricks under the legs of the cot (about 10 cm high). This helps them to keep their nose clear due to gravity. Keep them more upright as lying flat on a play-mat may be very uncomfortable; their nose is not easily drained when lying flat.

PYLORIC STENOSIS

This is a very rare condition with a narrowing at the far end of the stomach. It starts with projectile vomiting (vomit that misses your lap!), followed by being hungry for more feed and your baby becomes more miserable. It is usually noticeable between one to 11 weeks old and it is treated with surgery. Babies can vomit with some force which can be normal or may be linked to reflux.

REFLUX

Reflux is when the food in the stomach goes back up towards the mouth and causes problems such as irritability, back-arching or refusing to feed. Regurgitation and possetting is common in babies but it is reflux when it causes problems. Colic is not reflux (see **Colic**). Reflux generally starts between birth and three months and most resolve by 6 to 12 months.

Problems associated with reflux are: general irritability, back-arching; refusal to feed; recurrent cough; chestiness.

The treatment of reflux can be very difficult so I have given some ideas to try. Some will help while some will make no difference, so see what works for your baby. If your baby is not right, see your GP to discuss your baby's symptoms.

- Check volume of milk given at each feed. If you are bottle-feeding make sure you give your baby the amount recommended on side of formula packet and no more. You could even try feeding less at each feed but having one more feed a day to make up the total amount in a day. If you are breastfeeding this is difficult: you could try expressing a little off first and/or limiting the time allowed on the breast.
- Add a feed thickener if you are giving formula buy thickened anti-regurgitation formula or if you are breastfeeding then mix the thickener with a little expressed milk on a baby spoon or in a cup and give it first before your feed. Sometimes this can make the reflux worse not better!
- Elevate the head end of the cot slightly by putting 10 cm of books under the legs of the cot at the head end so gravity can help the food stay down.
- If you are using a formula, try changing it to a lactose-free or 'hydrolysed' formula -ask your doctor or pharmacist. Try the new formula for a week to see if makes a difference.
- See your GP for medicines to stop the acid in the stomach or to protect the stomach lining or for a medicine to help the stomach empty.

Most babies grow out of reflux so stop the medicines or changes every two to three months to see if your baby still needs it.

SKIN

When your baby is first born, their skin can be very dry and flaky. Do not peel; just leave your baby's own body to clear this on its own. If you want to start adding oils make sure they are very pure (no perfume added). Keep the products you use at bath-time to a minimum as their skin absorbs everything that touches it.

Jaundice

Look out for your baby looking yellow – yellow skin or yellow eyes. It is more common in premature babies and breastfed babies. Some breastfed babies can still be jaundiced at one month of age. The cause of the jaundice is generally harmless but there are a few serious diseases that need to be considered. If you are concerned ask your midwife or doctor. To monitor the jaundice a small blood test can be done to check your baby's 'bilirubin' levels to see if your baby needs treating or not. Treatment mainly involves keeping your baby well-hydrated and lying your baby under a bright light (phototherapy).

Birthmarks

Salmon patch/Stork mark

This is a flat pink/purple mark on the back of the neck. It can also be on the eyelids or between the eyebrows. In general it fades in the first two years.

Strawberry Naevus

This is a soft, bright red, raised lump that appears after a few days after birth. It is mainly on the head, neck or body. It usually enlarges in the first year or so then it goes away slowly; most have gone by five years old. They go without leaving a scar.

Port Wine Stain

This is flat and generally pale pink when first born. It then darkens with time to form a flat purple area. These do not fade with time. A paediatric assessment is needed if the Port Wine Stain is on the face or head. Some treatment options include camouflage makeup when they are older or laser treatment if advised.

Mongolian Blue Spot
These are large blue-grey spots mainly over the lower back and buttocks. They look like bruises. They are more common in darker skin than white skin. They tend to fade and most disappear by ten years old.

Moles
Some birthmarks are large moles. These are generally benign and rarely change or fade. Some have hair growing out of the darker area; this is normal. If it is a cosmetic problem then seek medical advice for an opinion. Most other moles appear after two years of age. If any mole changes shape, bleeds, changes colour or you are just concerned, always ask your doctor to look at it.

Rashes and spots

Milia (milk spots)
These are small yellow/white spots mainly on the face. These will go spontaneously.

Heat rash/red spots
These are areas of small red spots; they can look very bright, mainly on the face and in creases. Your baby will otherwise be well. Keep your baby's clothes dry, loose and cool. These also go spontaneously.

Spots inside the mouth
These are pearl-like spots on the roof of the mouth and will go spontaneously.

Dry skin

The occasional patch of dry skin is not eczema. The best way to treat it is to stop using any soap, shampoo or other products, and to add emulsifying oil (greasy lotion) to the bath; your pharmacist or doctor can recommend some for infants. Also, use a moisturising lotion or cream especially for dry skin in infants. It works best if you keep using the cream several times a day, for example with each nappy change.

Eczema

This usually starts in the cheeks, scalp and behind the ears. Cracks in the skin are typical of infantile eczema which is different from eczema as your baby will grow out of it. The rash can also be red, scaly, weeping, sore-looking and itchy. Please see your doctor for advice. There are lots of oils for the bath, ointments, creams or lotions for the skin and some will work for your baby and others will not. Topical steroids are used if the skin is very inflamed and itchy. At night (and for some by day) mittens or sleep suits with mittens folded over are great to prevent scratching. Make sure you keep their nails short so that if they get a chance to scratch they cannot do much harm. Use cotton for everything as this is the least irritating to skin, and try to avoid wool/lanolin. You may need to double-rinse their clothes as washing powder can be an irritant.

Dairy intolerance can be a reaction to the lactose (lactose intolerance) or the cow's milk protein.

If you are breastfeeding then try taking dairy products completely out of your own diet for two weeks, then reintroduce and see if your baby's skin has improved or if it changes when you start eating it again over the next three days. If it makes no difference, go back to eating dairy products again. Other common foods that may affect the skin are tomatoes, bananas and strawberries. If you are formula-feeding then try a lactose free formula or see your GP for a 'hydrolysed' formula milk for the allergic baby.

Once again try it for 2 weeks, provided your baby does not complain about the taste, and go back to your usual formula if it makes no difference.

To look out for milk products on labels you need to look for words on the packaging such as lactose, casein, caseinates, whey and actalbumin. Soya milk has a similar allergic effect to milk so is not recommended unless there are special reasons.

If your baby has eczema, avoid kissing him/her when you have a cold sore – or even when you feel one coming on – as this can cause a very severe skin reaction which will need treating.

Cradle Cap
This is a thick, light brown crust over the scalp. It can be very thick and looks very stuck on and is difficult to remove. Most pharmacists will sell medicated shampoo or cradle cap remover which can be very effective. Olive oil may work if mild. There are other creams containing salicylic acid and sulphur which you put on and rub before washing their hair which can be effective. Generally a comb or your fingernails is needed to help lift it off while using one of these products, but do not try to pick it off when it is dry as this will hurt.

SUDDEN INFANT DEATH SYNDROME (SIDS) or COT DEATH

SIDS or cot death is the sudden death of a well baby aged from birth to two years. Ninety per cent occur in the first six months. It is not possible to prevent a cot death but there are ways to decrease the risk significantly. SIDS is very rare and the following advice has proved to reduce the numbers even further.

The most important things to do to reduce the risk of cot death are:

- **Place your baby on their back to sleep (not side or stomach) in its own cot or crib.**

- **Do not smoke when pregnant and do not let anyone smoke in the same room as you or your baby.**

- **Do not use duvets, quilts, pillows or padded cot sides.**

- If you share a bed with your baby the risks of smothering your baby increases if you or your partner is extremely tired, if one of you smokes or if you are under the influence of alcohol, drugs or medication. This is especially important if your baby is small at birth, premature or under three months of age.

- Sofas and armchairs are not a suitable place for your baby to sleep.

- Do not let your baby get too hot: keep their head uncovered. Place your baby with their feet near the cot end so they cannot wriggle under the covers. Place the covers to their shoulders. Use lots of lightweight blankets to adjust to the temperature. Keep the room about 16-20°C. Your baby is too hot if it is sweating or its tummy feels too hot. Cold little hands are normal.

- Babies should never have a hot water bottle, electric blanket or be very near a radiator or heater or in direct sunlight.

- If you have no ventilation where your baby sleeps then a small fan in the room has recently been shown to help. Also avoid making your baby too cold.

- After five to six months it is common for babies to roll over. Still place your baby on its back to go to sleep, but you do not need to get up to check throughout the night.

THRUSH

Babies can have all, some or none of the following symptoms. They can start fidgeting while feeding or latching on and off frequently. They can become irritable and may also be more windy and difficult to settle. They can have white patches stuck to the cheeks, gums or tongue in their mouth. They can get a red and sore nappy rash. It is easily treatable so see your doctor for some medicine.

URINE INFECTIONS

Bladder/urine infections can often present in babies as an unexplained temperature, vomiting, diarrhoea, irritability, weight loss and/or generalised illness. It is important to collect a urine sample for your doctor. There are kits available to help which you place in the nappy otherwise you need to catch the urine in a sterile pot when it happens!

VACCINATIONS/IMMUNISATIONS

You will be given a list of immunisations your baby needs and the timings. I have tried to explain the reason to protect from these illnesses. Some of the following vaccines, which are part of childhood immunisations, prevent the majority of viral and bacterial causes of meningitis.

MMR

Measles, mumps and rubella are diseases with serious complications:

Measles can cause a range of symptoms as a result of the brain and nerve damage. It can be mild and just have a rash or when severe it can result in fits, deafness, loss of co-ordination, loss of concentration and memory, learning difficulties, lung, kidney and/or brain damage or in the very rare and worst cases death.

Mumps used to be the main cause of viral meningitis in children. It can cause temporary or permanent deafness, miscarriage, testicular swelling and, in rare cases, male infertility. There are 4 types of Mumps and the worst type is in the vaccine so if you do get Mumps having had the MMR it is generally only a mild infection.

Rubella mainly affects unborn babies resulting in miscarriages or congenital rubella syndrome which can cause deafness, blindness, heart defects or brain damage in the newborn.

There has been a lot of negative press associating the MMR vaccination with autism and bowel disease but no recent studies have proved the association. There has, however, been a huge reduction in meningitis, measles, mumps and congenital rubella syndrome as a result of the MMR. The vaccination program relies on something called herd immunity. The more people are immunised the less the disease is able to pass around. This then protects the vulnerable members of society who are unable to have the vaccine.

About seven to ten days after the MMR injection some children get a mild rash, fever and are a bit unwell for three to four days. About three to four weeks afterwards, some children may get a day or two of swollen glands. Other passing symptoms may be bruising all over or stiff joints. There is an option to give the MMR vaccine separately, but combining them decreases the number of injections that your baby receives and the research has not shown any benefits.

Meningitis C

Meningitis C used to cause a third of the cases of meningitis but is now very rare due to the new immunisations. This used to affect the under-2s and 18-25 year-olds.

DtaP/IPV/Hib vaccination

Diphtheria, tetanus, pertussis (whooping cough), polio and Haemophilus influenza type b.

Diphtheria is a serious disease which can damage the heart and nervous system and, in severe cases, it can kill.

Tetanus is a germ which attacks the nervous system and can lead to muscle spasm and breathing problems and can cause death.

Pertussis or Whooping Cough - (*see* **Coughs**).

Polio is a virus which attacks the nervous system and can cause permanent paralysis of muscles. If it affects the brain or chest muscles it can kill.

Hib virus is a known cause of meningitis as well as chest infections, arthritis and cellulitis.

Pneumo vaccination

This vaccine is to protect against pneumococcal infection which affects the very young (under-twos) and the very old. It can cause pneumonia (chest infection), septicaemia (blood poisoning), meningitis (inflammation around the brain) and peritonitis (inflammation of the abdomen). All these can cause death.

ESSENTIAL FIRST-AID

What to do if….

Your child gets scalded or burnt

If your baby gets even a small burn put the scalded area under **running cold water** (at least 10 to 20 minutes ideally if extensive) while you phone for medical help and wrap the area up in **clingfilm** while you travel to the hospital. If you can apply ice to it as well, such as a bag of frozen peas, this will help take the heat out.

If running cold water is not available then immerse the burnt area in any clean fluids such as water, milk or other cold drinks. Cover in a clean cloth if you do not have clingfilm. If the clothes are stuck to the skin do not try to take them off. If the burn is extensive, watch out for your child becoming faint and cold: lie your child down, keep them warm but not too hot. Do not prick blisters as this increases the likelihood of infection.

There are 3 types of burn depending on the severity:

Type 1 is superficial damage to the skin which turns red and is mildly painful.

Type 2 is where the burn has gone deeper into the skin and blisters appear. This is very painful.

Type 3 is a full thickness burn where the skin has gone leaving a hole which is white or charred black, this is less painful but more serious.

If the burn is Type 2 or 3 then go to your nearest hospital – preferably with a burns unit - especially if it is on your child's face, hands, arms or legs. The treatment available at Burns Units is now excellent and they will treat any sized burn even the smaller ones.

SUN

- The worst time of the day is between 11am and 3pm in the summer. Baby's skin can still burn before or after this time on a very hot day. A bit of morning or evening sun is good for them, however, to help make Vitamin D. Suntan lotion is not recommended for the newborn as it blocks absorption of vitamin D. Sun at any time of year can burn their delicate skin.

- Keep your baby in the shade as much as possible. If they are very young, less than six months, keep them in light cotton long sleeves and long legs and a hat.

- Always keep a hat on them. If it is very hot then a T-shirt with a collar is important and watch out for the back of their neck – a floppy hat or legionnaire-style hat can be very effective. Babies often keep pulling their hats off and refuse to wear them. Keep putting it back on again and again and they will eventually get the message. If they refuse to wear a hat then try to stay inside or in the shade during the heat of the day.

- Use children's suntan lotion – higher factor for younger babies but it is not recommended in the newborns.

- Car seats can be very hot when it is sunny so try to avoid driving in the heat for too long. There are window covers which are designed to decrease the amount of sunlight entering the car. Use the air conditioning if you have it and give them extra water to help avoid dehydration. If they are being breastfed they generally do not need extra water but bottle fed babies will need extra water either added to their normal bottle – add an extra 30mls of water or so for each feed or have some cooled boiled water in a separate bottle.

- Sunglasses have to have a regulated ultraviolet filter. If they do not have an ultraviolet filter, the sun may still harm the eyes as the glasses do not protect the eyes but also make the pupil of the eye open more to let more sunlight in.

- Use waterproof sun block if your child is swimming outside. Sun tops can be very protective, too.
- Reapply the sun block regularly throughout the day.
- Keep your child well-hydrated – they will need more water on a hot day than normal so keep offering water at intervals. If they suddenly go quiet or start crying for no reason offer them some water. Sometimes a little bit of sugar dissolved in the water can be more effective.
- Replace your sun creams yearly.
- The sunburn may not appear for up to 2 or so hours after being in the sun. The skin turns red, warm and painful with or without blisters. The pain lasts up to 48 hours then settles, the skin peels about 7 – 10 days later.

Treating Sunburn

Get your baby out of the sun!

- Either put your baby in a cool bath or wrap in cool damp towels. Repeat this regularly in the first few hours. Adding a small teaspoon of sodium bicarbonate to the bath water can be very soothing.
- If in a lot of pain give paracetamol and/or NSAID. Also an antihistamine if over 6 months of age unless under medical supervision.
- Offer fluids as the burn can cause dehydration.
- Do not apply butter, margarine, honey, petroleum jelly, warm water, tea bags or sunburn anaesthetic sprays.
- If there are no blisters then apply moisturising cream regularly.
- Wash blisters with mild soap and water, dry carefully and apply an antibiotic ointment and a sterile dressing.

Go to your family doctor or local Accident and Emergency if:

There are extensive burns
Skin blisters or open sores or if it looks infected
Fever greater than 38°C
Excessive sweating, babies may not be able to sweat so they are at a higher risk of 'heat stroke' and exhaustion
Signs of dehydration
Vomiting
Your baby just looks ill or unwell

Dehydration:
Dry mouth and tongue, cracked lips
Sunken eyes
Less urine than usual or no urine for 6 hours
The 'soft spot' on the top of the head is sunken/empty
Feet may be mottled or cold
Drowsy, listless

CHOKING
Call for urgent medical help

There are two sorts when an object is stuck in the airway:

- mild where your child is still breathing, crying and coughing
- severe where your child is unable to cough, cry or breathe

While waiting for help, if your child can still breathe and is staying calm then doing nothing and waiting for help can be a very safe option. If they can cough then encourage coughing as this is the most effective way to get the object out.

Alternatively:

- Do not try to remove the object because there is a high risk of pushing it down further making the problem worse.

- If **under one year old**, lay your baby over your forearm or your thigh with its head lower than its body and give five firm sharp **slaps** with the base of your hand between the shoulder blades. (Do not give abdominal thrusts to babies under one year old). Tilt their head back a little to open the airway.

- If your child is **over one year old** you could do five sharp slaps as above and if that does not work then try **abdominal thrusts** – stand behind your child, put your arms around them, and put the base/ heel of your hands at the top of the abdomen/tummy under the ribs and then pull quickly towards yourself going inwards and upwards under the rib cage. Repeat this five times.

- **If slaps and abdominal thrusts do not work do chest compressions.** Lie your child down on its back and give five chest thrusts/**compressions**, one finger width down from their nipple line if your baby is very small using 2 fingers to press down. If your child is bigger, use the base/heel of your hand on the area two fingers width above where the ribs meet. Then press down about a third of the depth of their chest. The idea is to try to shift the object with each chest compression.

- **If your child is not breathing** having given three cycles of back blows/abdominal thrusts and chest thrusts/compressions then **apply mouth to mouth ventilation/resuscitation** while waiting for urgent medical help to arrive. Be careful with mouth to mouth resuscitation/**rescue breaths** – you do not need to blow hard into your child's lungs as they are very small. You need to blow just enough to see the chest go up and down. If you do blow too hard then the rest of your air goes into their stomach and you risk causing them to vomit. Always tilt your child's head back a little to open the airways.

Paediatric Basic Life Support

ABC – Airways, Breathing, Circulation/Compressions

If your baby is unresponsive and not breathing give your baby five rescue breaths and then chest compressions (as described in '**Choking**' above). Do 30 chest compressions then two rescue breaths. Do this for one minute before going for help as the first minute is the most critical time for your baby. Your midwife often runs courses in Paediatric Life Support which you may like to attend.

OBJECTS STUCK UP NOSE/IN EARS/THROAT
Do not attempt to remove it yourself. Take your child to the nearest A&E department. Fish bones when stuck can be very painful and frightening but your child can still breathe so concentrate on distracting them and keeping them calm while seeking medical attention.

SWALLOWING POISONOUS SUBSTANCES
First try and work out exactly what and how much they have eaten. Check the floor around them for clues. If they have swallowed something you know is poisonous then go straight to your nearest Accident and Emergency Hospital. Take with you the box or label of the substance. If you are not sure how toxic or dangerous the product is then you most likely have time to phone for medical advice first or phone the company on the packet. If they have eaten a

mushroom - if you can find a similar looking mushroom take it with you to the hospital for identification.

If they have any soreness or blistering or staining around the mouth then give them a sip of milk or water on your way to the nearest hospital.

Dangerous signs are vomiting, drowsiness, pain, sweating and swelling. If they do stop breathing be prepared to give mouth to mouth resuscitation and chest thrusts (*see above* in choking).

If more Paracetamol is given or taken than the recommended amount in 24 hours it can reach toxic amounts very quickly especially in infants. Please get medical advice: paracetamol levels can be measured in blood which is an easy test to perform.

TOXIC PRODUCTS INTO EYES
Alkali products are the worst. **The most important thing to do is to wash it out,** either with their eye under running water such as a shower or to keep squeezing out a flannel over the eye. Encourage them to keep their eyes open if at all possible. Keep the running water going **for at least ten minutes** – get everything wet, the eye is more important than their clothes. If the eye is still stinging, or you are at all concerned, then go to your nearest Accident and Emergency Hospital.

STINGS – BEES AND WASPS
The bee leaves its sting in, the wasp does not. To pull out a bee sting use your nails to push it from under out rather than tweezers to pull it out as the tweezers may squeeze more poison in. Ammonia to the skin or antihistamine cream or oral antihistamine solution can help. Look out for severe allergic reactions such as swellings, wheeze, problems swallowing, headache or nausea. Any concerns then go to Accident and Emergency Hospital.

6: HOW TO BABY-PROOF YOUR HOME

This section is to inform you rather than to scare you and to make you aware of potential household dangers so you can prevent accidents.

- **Small objects** lying around on the floor can be put in their mouth and cause them to choke or suffocate. Be very careful especially if you have other children around as their toys may contain small parts.

- **Remove all strings or ribbons**, including those attached to certain toys – a child can tie these around their neck so quickly.

- **Keep plastic bags away** from babies as they may like putting things on their head.

- **Be careful of pets** and animals around your child. They are not always as reliable or predictable as you think.

- **Keep knives out of reach** – this sounds obvious but babies can often reach further than you expect.

- **Smoke detectors** – ensure they work and regularly test them.

- **Carbon Monoxide Alarms** – if you have flame-burning appliances or an open fire.

- **Lock up all domestic cleaning fluids** – preferably out of reach too. The tablets for dishwashing machines are very dangerous either if eaten or rubbed into their eyes and their shiny packaging makes them look attractive to children.

- **All medicines have to be out of reach** – preferably in a locked cupboard up high. You can fit catches or locks or you can just make sure that nothing within their reach will harm them.

- **Furniture straps** – this is more for the toddlers, to attach chests of drawers and cupboards to the wall so if pulled on they are not able to fall forward onto your child.

- **Curtains** – make sure the sash cords/strings to pull the curtains open and shut are out of reach. Avoid having a loop if possible. It is amazing how easily babies can get themselves dangerously tangled up.

- **Plugs** – use safety plugs, even though your baby will not be on the move for a few months. Also check you have no worn flexes or flexes dangling down off work surfaces.

- **Hide breakable items** – put them away for a few years or be prepared for the odd breakage.

- **Tape sharp corners** especially when your child is learning to crawl or walk.

- **Stair gates** – at the top and bottom of the stairs when they can crawl.

- **Windows** must have safety catches so your baby cannot crawl out or fall out. However, also think about how you would get out of your house if you have a fire.

- **Glass indoors** – change it to safety glass or board it up.

- Do not let your baby crawl or walk with **sharp objects in their hands or anything in their mouth** such as toothbrushes.

- **Keep alcohol away** from them.

- **Irons** – never leave the iron even for a second when it is on, and preferably avoid doing the ironing when your baby is awake. Make sure the flex is not dangling down.

- **Hair straighteners** get very hot so be careful where you leave them before and after doing your hair.

- **Cooking** – turn **pan handles** inwards, try to use the back rings as much as possible and be extra careful if your baby is under your feet. Think about where you put your **cup of tea or coffee**: do not leave your cup on a table cloth, for example, which can be pulled. Shorten the **kettle flex** so it cannot be pulled down.

- **Microwave** – remember the uneven distribution of heat so stir whatever you've heated well and double-check before serving

- **Bath water** – if you are putting a child in the bath it is your responsibility to check the temperature, not the person who ran the bath. There are lots of bath thermometers around – otherwise use your elbow to test the water rather than your hands.

- **Fire or gas heaters** – fire guards need to be fixed to the wall and to surround the heater completely

- Beware of **hot oven frames/fronts**

- Keep **matches** in a safe place

- **Do not have hot water bottles or electric blankets in the cot**

Water: Baths, paddling pools and ponds – **never leave your baby or child unattended by water** even for a short time. Also remember you are always more off-guard when you are with another person or group or in someone else's house.

Enjoy the experience of having a new baby in your life.

May you relish the ups and sail through the downs!

THIS TIME IS VERY SPECIAL.

DISCLAIMER

Illustrations by Elinor B. Greenacre

www.elinordesigns.co.uk

Published in the UK by DragonWeb Publishing Ltd

73 Greville Road, Bristol BS3 1LE

www.DragonWebPublishing.com

2506304R00090

Printed in Great Britain
by Amazon.co.uk, Ltd.,
Marston Gate.